the complete series

CUPCAKES

hinkler

Published by Hinkler Books Pty Ltd
45–55 Fairchild Street
Heatherton Victoria 3202 Australia
www.hinkler.com.au

hinkler

Text and images © Anthony Carroll 2010
Design © Hinkler Books Pty Ltd 2011

Cover design: Hinkler Design Studio
Typesetting: MPS Limited
Prepress: Graphic Print Group

ISBN: 978 1 7418 4130 5

Printed and bound in China

CONTENTS

INTRODUCTION

Baking cupcakes is a pleasurable and rewarding experience, not just for you, the home cook, but also for those who gather to enjoy the fruits of your labour. So quick and delicious, they can be made when friends drop in, or just on a whim on a lazy afternoon.

Ease and simplicity have always been part of making cupcakes. Once upon a time, back in the early 1800s, they were called 'measure cakes' or 'number cakes' as well as cupcakes because the ingredients were measured by cup, not using a set of scales. It was a quicker way of preparing the recipe during a time when afternoon teas were a way of life. They also derive their name from the fact they were often cooked in a teacup. Teacups, often the second-best ones, would be greased, filled with a simple batter (similar to a pound cake) and baked in a wood- or coal-fired stove. Because the cupcakes were smaller than a normal cake, they required less fuel and less time to cook; perfect for a thrifty housewife!

The recipe for the cupcake has remained a fairly simple affair (although it's rare these days to see someone cooking them in old teacups). However, they have evolved to become something slightly more elegant. They're a way for the inventive cook to show off their talents and imagination, from the simple beauty of a plain cupcake with white icing and a glacé (glazed) cherry, to a beautifully decorated little cake with dark chocolate ganache and butter icing flowers. To many people, a batch of cupcakes is a blank canvas on which to paint and decorate, to show their true artistic talents – to others they remain simply a fast, delicious cake.

Preparation

Before you start making cupcakes (or any recipe for that matter) it's important to make sure you have all the ingredients and equipment on hand.

First, take a little time to read the recipe from the beginning to end. Although a lot of the recipes in this book use similar methods, there may be subtle differences. Next, check through the ingredients and make sure you have enough of each. There's nothing worse than starting a recipe only to find you have to go down the street for more sugar!

Allow farm ingredients stored in the refrigerator, such as butter and eggs, to come to room temperature before using: cold ingredients can cause the mix to contract and become tough.

Many people prefer the rich flavour and moist texture that full-fat milk gives to their cooking, although the more health-conscious will prefer to use skimmed

or low-fat milk. Either way, once again the milk should be at room temperature. Some people like to measure out the required amount of milk, cover it with plastic wrap and leave it out to come to room temperature, so they can return the rest to the refrigerator to keep fresh.

Cupcake papers or cases are little paper cups with pleated edges, in which the cupcake batter can be poured and then put in the oven for baking. Quality cupcake papers are a boon. Look for ones with thick paper that will keep their shape during time in the oven. Thin papers don't hold their shape which can result in a wasteful mess of baked mix and paper! To avoid this, papers are best dropped into a cupcake tray, which will keep everything perfectly in place.

If you don't have a cupcake tray, place the papers on an ovenproof tray – this will keep them together and stop any spills from spoiling the bottom of the oven. Position the papers closely together, so they can help each other hold their shape.

If you plan on doing a lot of baking, it's a good idea to spend a little extra money and get a good, durable cupcake tray. Grease the trays well before you bake, and make sure they're not hot, as this can start the baking process too early!

Almost time to turn on the oven!

The tradition of home baking has always been about putting good food on the table. When the cakes are brought out and the tea or coffee is served, it's an occasion for family, neighbours and friends to take time to sit down and talk, to be with each other and to listen, laugh, remember old times and plan new events. The smell of freshly baked goods, the perfumes of spice wafting through the air will create an environment of gentle anticipation of pleasure and excitement for the young and the young at heart.

To create the perfect cupcake, time after time, there are a few simple rules to follow:

- Sift the dry ingredients together and make sure they are mixed through thoroughly. Lumps in the flour in the early stages can cause hard lumps to end up in the final mix, which is not a desirable outcome.

- Nuts make nutritious, energy-packed highlights and a delicious crowning glory for a cupcake. To get the premium flavour from nuts, ensure they're fresh and give them a gentle toasting in a warm oven for a few minutes to bring out their flavours. Evenly spread the nuts over an ovenproof tray covered with oven paper. Toast almonds and hazelnuts at 180°C (350°F) for 10 minutes. Walnuts and pecans should be toasted a little more gently, at 160°C (320°F) for 10 minutes, and macadamias at 150°C (300°F) for the same period. Keep an eye on the nuts as you toast them, as they can change colour and burn very rapidly if left unattended. They should develop a lovely golden hue, but nothing darker.

- Do not over-work the mix beyond the time recommended in the method of the recipe. This makes the proteins in the flour (ie gluten) stick together, meaning the mix will be too strong and tough and won't rise. The lightest touch possible should be used!

- Remember to not overload the cupcakes with extra fillings – sometimes it can be too much of a good thing! Fold in added ingredients such as chocolate and nuts after the batter is made, to help distribute them evenly. If you add the fillings to the dry ingredients, the flour will stick to the nuts or bits of chocolate, stopping them from becoming part of the dough.

- There's nothing worse than biting into a cupcake to find that all the ingredients have unexpectedly sunk to the bottom.

- To make cleaning a lot easier, a little bit of cooking oil can be used to coat utensils before use. A cheese grater, if lightly brushed with a neutral cooking oil such as canola or sunflower seed oil, will clean up much more easily. If you plan on using honey, maple syrup, golden syrup or treacle, a little oil brushed on the cup or measuring spoon will stop the sticky liquid from adhering, making for a more accurate measure and less time at the sink.

- When baking, note that not all ovens are the same and that cooking times can vary. In non-fan-forced ovens, the cupcakes on the inside of the tray take slightly longer to cook, so by the time they are ready the ones on the outside may be slightly deeper golden. A good rule of thumb is to insert a fine skewer into the cupcake – if it's ready, the skewer will come out clean. With experience you'll be able to judge with your eyes and nose when they are baked to perfection.

Cupcakes are at their best fresh after cooling on a wire rack. When decorating, handle the cupcakes by their base, as this is their strongest point.

With decorating, there's no right or wrong. You'll need a spatula and plenty of fresh warm water to sculpt and spread the icing (frosting) across the top of the cupcake. For applying icing in patterns, you can start off using a sturdy plastic bag with a tiny hole snipped off one corner – it's rough and ready, but OK to get you started. You'll have more control with a good icing bag, or gun and a set of nozzles. Some nozzles are cut and moulded to allow the production of flowers and leaves and other shapes. Value-for-money icing kits can be purchased from good food stores and department stores. Make sure your nozzles are cleaned properly straight after use, as set icing is harder to clean than fresh.

Chocolate is a joy to eat and a popular decoration. Melted dark chocolate can be used to drizzle delectable contrasting patterns over white icing.

Chocolate can be melted in a ceramic cup in the microwave, but the traditional method is still the best. Break the chocolate up into small pieces and put it in a heatproof bowl sitting on top of a saucepan containing barely simmering hot water (a bain-marie or double-boiler). Stir the chocolate as it melts. Never ever let water get into the chocolate, as this will cause it to become granular. If you do end up with water in your chocolate, add a dash of cooking oil to help the chocolate return to the desired texture.

On the following page, we've included a basic explanation of how to prepare a piping bag. It's a handy skill if you have a piece of baking paper around, but if you find it a bit fiddly, or you don't have any paper on hand, the back-up trick is to fill the corner of a small plastic bag, simply roll it up and snip off the point. As long as the bag is sturdy enough and the person controlling the piping is gentle enough, the humble plastic bag can work wonderfully for applying line decorations or writing messages on individual cakes.

Once you've made a few of these recipes, you'll find the ones that you love and come back to time and time again. They'll become your family favourites! You might even want to experiment by changing the decorations, the flavourings or toppings. You'll have cakes that you've made with skill in your own kitchen, that will please friends and family and when you have your favourite recipes they can be made for unexpected guests at the drop of the hat.

Preparing a plastic bag for piping

1 Take a sturdy, small- to medium-sized plastic bag, place the icing or warm chocolate into one corner and gently remove any air from the bag.

2 Fold over then roll down the top of the plastic bag on a diagonal angle, toward the filled corner.

3 Snip a small piece of plastic from the corner of the bag to allow the icing to flow. Control the icing by applying more or less pressure to the rolled-up back part of the bag.

Making a paper piping bag

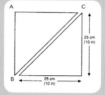

1 Cut a 25cm (10in) square of greaseproof paper. Cut the square in half diagonally to form two triangles. To make the piping bag, place the paper triangles on top of each other and mark the three corners A, B and C.

2 Fold corner B around and inside corner A.

3 Bring corner C around the outside of the bag until it fits exactly behind corner A. At this stage all three corners should be together and the point closed.

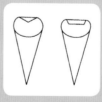

4 Fold corner A over two or three times to hold the bag together. Snip the point off the bag and drop in an icing nozzle. The piping bag can also be used without a nozzle for writing and outlines; in which case, only the very tip of the point should be snipped off.

VANILLA & COFFEE
CUPCAKES

VANILLA & COFFEE CUPCAKES

Recipes in this chapter cover the original vanilla cupcake with traditional toppings, as well as yummy coffee flavourings!

WHITE CHOC MOCHA CUPCAKES

2 eggs
125g (4.4oz) butter, softened
1 cup caster (berry) sugar
½ cup milk
2 cups self-raising flour, sifted
100g (3.5oz) white chocolate, grated
2 teaspoon instant coffee powder
Topping
1½ cups icing (confectioner's) sugar
125g (4.4oz) butter, softened
1 teaspoon instant coffee powder
white chocolate curls to decorate

1   Preheat the oven to 160°C (320°F). Line a 12-cupcake pan with cupcake papers. In a medium-sized bowl, lightly beat the eggs, add butter and sugar, then mix until light and fluffy.

2   Add the milk, flour, chocolate and coffee, and stir to combine. Beat with an electric mixer for 2 minutes, until light and creamy.

3   Divide the mixture evenly between the cake papers. Bake for 18–20 minutes until risen and firm to touch. Allow to cool for a few minutes and then transfer to a wire rack. Allow to cool fully before icing (frosting).

Topping

1   Meanwhile, combine the icing (confectioner's) sugar, butter and coffee; beat with a wooden spoon until light and fluffy.

2   Spoon topping onto cupcakes, using the back of a spoon, then add decorations.

Makes 12 · Preparation 12 minutes · Cooking 20 minutes

DOUBLE VANILLA CUPCAKES

2 eggs
125g (4.4oz) butter, softened
1 cup caster (berry) sugar
½ cup buttermilk
2 cups self-raising flour, sifted
1 teaspoon vanilla extract
Topping
1½ cups icing (confectioner's) sugar
125g (4.4oz) butter, softened
seeds scraped from 1 vanilla bean

1   Preheat the oven to 160°C (320°F). Line a 12-cupcake pan with cupcake papers. In a medium-sized bowl, lightly beat the eggs, add butter and sugar, then mix until light and fluffy.

2   Add buttermilk, flour and vanilla, and stir to combine. Beat with an electric mixer for 2 minutes, until light and creamy.

3   Divide the mixture evenly between the cake papers. Bake for 18–20 minutes until risen and firm to touch. Allow to cool for a few minutes and then transfer to a wire rack. Allow to cool fully before icing (frosting).

Topping

1   Meanwhile, combine half the topping ingredients except vanilla bean seeds and stir with a wooden spoon until mixed together. Add remaining ingredients and beat with the spoon until light and fluffy.

2   Spoon topping onto cakes using the back of a spoon.

Makes 12 · Preparation 12 minutes · Cooking 20 minutes

WHITE CHOCOLATE AND SOUR CREAM CUPCAKES

2 eggs
125g (4.4oz) butter, softened
1 cup caster (berry) sugar
½ cup sour cream
2 cups self-raising flour, sifted
1 teaspoon vanilla extract
Topping
100g (3.5oz) white chocolate, coarsely grated
1 tablespoon butter, softened
⅓ cup thickened (whipping) cream
Sugar (candy) flowers (available from cake decorating shops)

1   Preheat the oven to 160°C (320°F). Line a 12-cupcake pan with cupcake papers. In a medium-sized bowl, lightly beat the eggs, add butter and sugar, then mix until light and fluffy.

2   Add sour cream, flour and vanilla, and stir to combine. Beat with an electric mixer for 2 minutes, until light and creamy.

3   Divide the mixture evenly between the cake papers. Bake for 18–20 minutes until risen and firm to touch. Allow to cool for a few minutes and then transfer to a wire rack. Allow to cool fully before icing (frosting).

Topping

1   Meanwhile, combine the chocolate and butter in a medium-sized saucepan over a medium heat. As the mixture begins to melt, add the cream slowly, then reduce heat to low, stirring constantly, until mixture thickens.

2   Remove from heat and cool. Spread evenly onto cupcakes with a teaspoon, then top with flower decorations.

Makes 12 · Preparation 12 minutes · Cooking 20 minutes

PERSIAN VANILLA SAFFRON CUPCAKES

2 eggs
125g (4.4oz) butter, softened
1 cup caster (berry) sugar
½ cup milk
2 cups self-raising flour, sifted
1 teaspoon vanilla extract
1 pinch saffron strands
Topping
1½ cups icing (confectioner's) sugar
1 teaspoon lemon extract
1 teaspoon vanilla extract
125g (4.4oz) butter, softened
Persian fairy (candy) floss

1   Preheat the oven to 160°C (320°F). Line a 12-cupcake pan with cupcake papers. In a medium-sized bowl, lightly beat the eggs, add butter and sugar, then mix until light and fluffy.

2   Add milk, flour, vanilla and saffron then stir to combine. Beat with an electric mixer for 2 minutes, until light and creamy.

3   Divide the mixture evenly between the cake papers. Bake for 18–20 minutes until risen and firm to touch. Allow to cool for a few minutes and then transfer to a wire rack. Allow to cool fully before icing (frosting).

Topping

1   Meanwhile, combine all topping ingredients except fairy (candy) floss, mix with a wooden spoon until well combined, and beat with the spoon until light and fluffy.

2   Place mixture into a piping bag with a star-shaped nozzle and pipe onto all cupcakes. Top with fairy floss.

Makes 12 · Preparation 12 minutes · Cooking 20 minutes

Vanilla snowflake cupcakes

2 eggs
125g (4.4oz) butter, softened
1 cup caster (berry) sugar
½ cup milk
2 cups self-raising flour, sifted
1 teaspoon vanilla extract
Topping
1½ cups icing (confectioner's) sugar
125g (4.4oz) butter, softened
white sprinkles to decorate

1   Preheat the oven to 160°C (320°F). Line a 12-cupcake pan with cupcake papers. In a medium-sized bowl, lightly beat the eggs, add butter and sugar, then mix until light and fluffy.

2   Add milk, flour and vanilla, and stir to combine. Beat with an electric mixer for 2 minutes, until light and creamy.

3   Divide the mixture evenly between the cake papers. Bake for 18–20 minutes until risen and firm to touch. Allow to cool for a few minutes and then transfer to a wire rack. Allow to cool fully before icing (frosting).

Topping

1   Meanwhile, combine half the icing (confectioner's) sugar and butter, mix with a wooden spoon, add the remaining icing sugar and butter and beat with the spoon until light and fluffy.

2   Use a piping bag fitted with a round nozzle to pipe the toping onto the cupcakes. Top with white sprinkles.

Makes 12 · Preparation 12 minutes · Cooking 20 minutes

VANILLA ROSE PETAL CUPCAKES

2 eggs
125g (4.4oz) butter, softened
1 cup caster (berry) sugar
½ cup milk
2 cups self-raising flour, sifted
1 teaspoon vanilla extract
Topping
1½ cups icing (confectioner's) sugar
1 teaspoon rose water
125g (4.4oz) butter, softened
6 drops vanilla extract
rose petals to decorate (available from cake decoration stores)

1 Preheat the oven to 160°C (320°F). Line a 12-cupcake pan with cupcake papers. In a medium-sized bowl, lightly beat the eggs, add butter and sugar, then mix until light and fluffy.

2 Add milk, flour and vanilla, and stir to combine. Beat with an electric mixer for 2 minutes, until light and creamy.

3 Divide the mixture evenly between the cake papers. Bake for 18–20 minutes until risen and firm to touch. Allow to cool for a few minutes and then transfer to a wire rack. Allow to cool fully before icing (frosting).

Topping

1 Meanwhile, combine half of all the topping ingredients except roses petals, mix with a wooden spoon, add remaining ingredients and beat with the spoon until light and fluffy.

2 Place mixture into a piping bag with a plain nozzle and pipe onto cupcakes. Decorate with rose petals.

Makes 12 • Preparation 12 minutes • Cooking 20 minutes

MOCHA CHOC CHIP CUPCAKES

2 eggs
125g (4.4oz) butter, softened
1 cup caster (berry) sugar
½ cup milk
1 teaspoon vanilla extract
2 cups self-raising flour, sifted
2 tablespoons instant coffee
½ cup mini chocolate chips
Topping
1½ cups icing (confectioner's) sugar
125g (4.4oz) butter, softened
1 teaspoon instant coffee
mini chocolate chips to decorate

1　Preheat the oven to 160°C (320°F). Line a 12-cupcake pan with cupcake papers. In a medium sized bowl, lightly beat the eggs, add butter and sugar, then mix until light and fluffy.

2　Add milk, vanilla, flour and coffee, stir to combine. Beat with an electric mixer for 2 minutes until light and fluffy. Stir through the chocolate chips.

3　Divide the mixture between the cake papers. Bake for 18–20 minutes until risen and firm to the touch. Allow to cool for a few minutes, then transfer to a wire rack. Allow to cool fully before icing (frosting).

Topping

1　Mix together the icing (confectioner's) sugar, butter and coffee until well combined, then beat until light and fluffy.

2　Use a piping bag fitted with a star nozzle to pipe the topping onto the cupcakes. Decorate with chocolate chips.

Makes 12 · Preparation 12 minutes · Cooking 20 minutes

COFFEE WALNUT CUPCAKES

2 cups self-raising flour, sifted
¼ cup chopped walnuts
125g (4.4oz) butter, softened
1 cup caster (berry) sugar
2 teaspoons instant coffee
2 eggs
½ cup milk
Topping
1 cup icing (confectioner's) sugar
1 teaspoon instant coffee
2–3 tablespoons boiling water
12 whole walnut halves

1   Preheat the oven to 200°C (400°F). Line 12-cupcake pan with cupcake papers.

2   Combine the flour and walnuts in a medium-sized bowl. Beat the butter, sugar and coffee in a large bowl until creamy. Add the eggs, one at a time, until just blended. Fold in the dry ingredients and milk.

3   Divide the mixture evenly between the cake papers. Bake for 12–15 minutes until risen and firm to touch. Allow to cool for a few minutes and then transfer to a wire rack. Allow to cool fully before icing (frosting).

Topping

1   Combine the icing (confectioner's) sugar and coffee, and mix with enough water to make a soft icing.

2   Apply icing to each cupcake with a knife and top each cupcake with a walnut half.

Makes 12 cupcakes · Preparation 10 minutes · Cooking 15 minutes

SPICED COFFEE CREAM CUPCAKES

125g (4.4oz) butter, softened
1 cup icing (berry) sugar
2 eggs
½ cup milk
2 cups self-raising flour, sifted
¾ cup coffee beans, very finely ground
1 teaspoon allspice
Topping
2 cups whipped cream
allspice for dusting

1　Preheat the oven to 180°C (350°F). Line a 12-cupcake pan with cupcake papers. In a medium bowl combine and beat butter, sugar and eggs until light and fluffy. Add milk and flour and stir to combine. Add remaining ingredients and mix well.

2　Divide the mixture evenly between the cake papers. Bake for 15–20 minutes until cakes are cooked. Allow to cool completely before decorating.

3　Spoon the cream on top of each cupcake and dust with allspice.

Makes 12 · Preparation 15 minutes · Cooking 20 minutes

COFFEE AND HAZELNUT CUPCAKES

125g (4.4oz) butter, softened
½ cup milk
½ tablespoon instant coffee
2 eggs
1 cup caster (berry) sugar
2 cups self-raising flour, sifted
½ cup hazelnuts, chopped
Topping
1½ cups icing (confectioner's) sugar
2 tablespoons instant coffee
125g (4.4oz) butter, softened
4 drops vanilla extract
hazelnuts, chopped and toasted to decorate
icing (confectioner's) sugar and cocoa powder, for dusting

1 Preheat the oven to 180°C (350°F). Line a 12-cupcake pan with cupcake papers. In a saucepan, heat the butter, milk and coffee gently and stir until butter is melted. Allow to cool.

2 In a large bowl, whisk the eggs with an electric mixer until thick and creamy. Add the sugar gradually, then stir in half the butter mixture and flour and beat. Add the remaining butter mixture and flour and beat until smooth. Add the hazelnuts and stir through gently.

3 Divide the mixture evenly between the cake papers. Bake for 20 minutes until risen and firm to touch. Allow to cool for a few minutes and then transfer to a wire rack. Allow to cool fully before icing (frosting).

Topping

1 Meanwhile, combine the first four topping ingredients in a medium-sized bowl and beat slowly with an electric mixer for 1 minute. Turn speed up and beat until light and fluffy.

2 Place mixture into a piping bag and pipe onto cupcakes, sprinkle with hazelnuts and dust with icing (confectioner's) sugar and cocoa powder.

Makes 12 · Preparation 20 minutes · Cooking 20 minutes

COFFEE ALMOND CUPCAKES

2 eggs
125g (4.4oz) butter, softened
1 cup caster (berry) sugar
½ cup milk
1 cup self-raising flour, sifted
¼ teaspoon baking powder
½ cup ground almonds (almond meal)
½ cup almonds, chopped
¼ cup cocoa powder
3 tablespoons instant coffee
Topping
1½ cups icing (confectioner's) sugar
125g (4.4oz) unsalted butter, softened
1 teaspoon almond extract
1 teaspoon instant coffee
36 chocolate coffee beans

1   Preheat the oven to 160°C (320°F). Line a 12-cupcake pan with cupcake papers. In a medium-sized bowl, lightly beat the eggs, add butter and sugar, then mix until light and fluffy.

2   Add milk and flour, and stir to combine. Add remaining cake ingredients. Mix with a wooden spoon for 2 minutes, until light and creamy.

3   Divide the mixture evenly between the cake papers. Bake for 18–20 minutes until risen and firm to touch. Allow to cool for a few minutes, and then transfer to a wire rack. Allow to cool fully before icing (frosting).

Topping

1   Meanwhile, combine all topping ingredients except for coffee beans in a small bowl and mix with a wooden spoon.

2   Spoon onto cupcakes with the back of the spoon and decorate each cake with three chocolate coffee beans.

Makes 12 · Preparation 12 minutes · Cooking 20 minutes

FRENCH COFFEE CUPCAKES

125g (4.4oz) butter, softened
¼ cup milk
2 tablespoons milk powder
1 tablespoon instant coffee
2 eggs
1 cup caster (berry) sugar
2 cups self-raising flour, sifted
½ cup Grand Marnier
Topping
1½ cups icing (confectioner's) sugar
¼ cup milk powder
125g (4.4oz) butter, softened
1 tablespoon Grand Marnier
Crystallised (candied) orange zest to decorate

1   Preheat the oven to 180°C (350°F). Line a 12-cupcake pan with cupcake papers. In a saucepan, heat the butter, milk, milk powder and coffee gently and stir until butter is melted. Allow to cool.

2   In a large bowl, whisk the eggs with an electric mixer until thick and creamy. Add the sugar gradually, then stir in half the butter mixture and flour and beat. Add the Grand Marnier, then the remaining butter mixture and flour and beat until smooth.

3   Divide the mixture evenly between the cake papers. Bake for 20 minutes until risen and firm to touch. Allow to cool for a few minutes and then transfer to a wire rack. Allow to cool fully before icing (frosting).

Topping

1   Meanwhile, combine all of the ingredients except the Grand Marnier and orange zest in a medium-sized bowl and beat with an electric mixer for 1 minute. Turn speed up and beat until light and fluffy. Add the Grand Marnier slowly and mix again until thoroughly combined.

2   Place mixture into a piping bag and pipe onto all cupcakes. Sprinkle with the orange zest.

Makes 12 · Preparation 20 minutes · Cooking 20 minutes

PECAN PRALINE CUPCAKES

2 eggs
125g (4.4oz) butter, softened
1 cup caster (berry) sugar
½ cup milk
2 cups self-raising flour, sifted
1 tablespoon espresso coffee
½ cup pecans, chopped
1 tablespoon golden syrup
Topping
200g (7oz) sugar
125g (4.4oz) butter, softened
100g (35oz) pecans, chopped
1½ cups icing (confectioner's) sugar

1 Preheat the oven to 160°C (320°F). Line a 12-cupcake pan with cupcake papers. In a medium-sized bowl, lightly beat the eggs, add butter and sugar, then mix until light and fluffy.

2 Add milk and flour, and stir to combine. Add remaining ingredients. Mix with a wooden spoon for 2 minutes, until light and creamy.

3 Divide the mixture evenly between the cake papers. Bake for 18–20 minutes until risen and firm to touch. Allow to cool for a few minutes, then transfer to a wire rack. Allow to cool fully before icing (frosting).

Topping

1 Meanwhile, combine sugar, half the butter and 100ml (3.4 fl oz) water in a saucepan, bring to the boil and simmer over a medium heat until the mixture becomes a golden colour. Stir in pecans and quickly pour onto an oiled tray. Allow to cool and harden before breaking into pieces.

2 Beat together icing (confectioner's) sugar and remaining butter until light and fluffy. Use a piping bag fitted with a plain nozzle to pipe the icing onto the cupcakes. Decorate with praline pieces.

Makes 12 · Preparation 12 minutes · Cooking 20 minutes

Italian coffee cupcakes

125g (4.4oz) butter, softened
½ cup milk, scalded then cooled
½ teaspoon vanilla extract
2 eggs
1 cup caster (berry) sugar
2 cups self-raising flour, sifted
1½ tablespoons skim milk powder
1 tablespoon instant coffee
2 tablespoons Amaretto
Topping
1½ cups icing (confectioner's) sugar
½ cup milk powder
1 tablespoon instant coffee
100g (3.5oz) butter, softened
2 tablespoons milk
4 drops vanilla extract
2 tablespoons Amaretto
cocoa powder to dust

1 Preheat the oven to 180°C (350°F). Line a 12-cupcake pan with cupcake papers.
   In a saucepan, heat the butter, ¼ cup of milk and vanilla gently and stir until butter
   is melted. Add the remaining milk and allow to cool.

2 In a large bowl, whisk the eggs with an electric mixer until thick and creamy.
   Add the sugar gradually, then stir in half the butter mixture and half of the flour
   and beat. Add the remaining butter mixture, flour, skim milk powder, coffee and
   Amaretto and beat until smooth.

3 Divide the mixture evenly between the cake papers. Bake for 20 minutes until
   risen and firm to touch. Allow to cool for a few minutes and then transfer to a
   wire rack. Allow to cool fully before icing (frosting).

Topping

1 Meanwhile, combine all of the topping ingredients except the cocoa powder in
   a medium-sized bowl and beat with an electric mixer on slow for 1 minute. Turn
   speed up and beat for 5 minutes until light and fluffy.

2 Place mixture into a piping bag, pipe onto all cupcakes and dust with cocoa powder.

Makes 12 · Preparation 20 minutes · Cooking 20 minutes

MORNING COFFEE CUPCAKES

2 cups self-raising flour, sifted
4½ tablespoons instant coffee
125g (4.4oz) butter, softened
¼ teaspoon vanilla extract
1 cup caster (berry) sugar
2 eggs
¼ cup milk
¼ cup Amaretto
Topping
1½ cups icing (confectioner's) sugar
½ cup milk powder
100g (3.5oz) butter, softened
2 tablespoons milk
4 drops vanilla extract
1 tablespoon instant coffee

1   Preheat the oven to 180°C (350°F). Line a 12-cupcake pan with cupcake papers.
    Sift the dry ingredients together.

2   In a medium-sized bowl, beat the butter, vanilla and sugar with an electric mixer
    until creamy. Add the eggs one at a time and beat until well combined.

3   Add the dry ingredients, milk and Amaretto to the butter mixture and
    combine thoroughly.

4   Divide the mixture evenly between the cake papers. Bake for approximately
    20 minutes until risen and firm to touch. Allow to cool for a few minutes and then
    transfer to a wire rack. Allow to cool fully before icing (frosting).

Topping

1   Meanwhile, combine all of the topping ingredients except the instant coffee in a
    medium-sized bowl and beat with an electric mixer on slow for 1 minute. Turn
    speed up and beat until light and fluffy. Add 1 teaspoon of water to the coffee and
    add to the topping, stirring only once.

2   Spread topping evenly onto cupcakes with the back of a teaspoon.

Makes 12 · Preparation 20 minutes · Cooking 20 minutes

MINI CUPCAKES,
KIDS

MINI CUPCAKES, KIDS

For that quick one-time snack for the kids, try mini cupcakes with a multitude of flavoured toppings, all guaranteed to keep the little ones happy. The toppings are all very innovative and look great on a party table.

Fairy mini cupcakes

80g (2.8oz) butter, softened
½ cup caster (berry) sugar
1 egg
1 cup self-raising flour, sifted
⅓ cup milk
½ teaspoon vanilla extract
½ teaspoon pink food colouring
Topping
1 cup icing (confectioner's) sugar
2 tablespoons hot water
rainbow sprinkles, to decorate

1   Preheat the oven to 160°C (320°F). Line a 24 mini cupcake pan with mini cupcake papers. In a medium-sized bowl, use an electric mixer on high speed to cream the butter and sugar until light and fluffy. Add the egg and mix well.

2   Add the flour, milk, vanilla and pink colouring, and beat with an electric mixer on medium until well combined.

3   Divide the mixture evenly between the 24 mini cupcake papers. Bake for 10–15 minutes until well risen and firm to the touch. Allow to cool for a few minutes and then transfer to a wire rack. Allow to cool fully before icing (frosting).

Topping

1   Mix the icing (confectioner's) sugar with hot water until well combined and smooth. Spread evenly over each mini cupcake and sprinkle with rainbow sprinkles.

Makes 24 · Preparation 20 minutes · Cooking 15 minutes

CARNIVAL MINI CUPCAKES

80g (2.8oz) butter, softened
½ cup caster (berry) sugar
1 egg
1 cup self-raising flour, sifted
⅓ cup milk
½ teaspoon vanilla extract
Topping
80g (2.8oz) butter, softened
1 cup icing (confectioner's) sugar
mini coated chocolate buttons, to decorate

1 Preheat the oven to 160°C (320°F). Line a 24 mini cupcake pan with mini cupcake papers. In a medium-sized bowl, use an electric mixer on high speed to cream the butter and sugar until light and fluffy. Add the egg and mix well.

2 Add the flour, milk and vanilla, and beat with an electric mixer on medium until well combined.

3 Divide the mixture evenly between the 24 mini cupcake papers. Bake for 10–15 minutes until well risen and firm to the touch. Allow to cool for a few minutes and then transfer to a wire rack. Allow to cool fully before icing (frosting).

Topping

1 Use an electric mixer on high speed to beat the butter until light and fluffy. Gradually beat in icing (confectioner's) sugar until all combined, continue beating for 1 minute. Spread evenly over each cupcake and decorate with the chocolate buttons.

Makes 24 · Preparation 20 minutes · Cooking 15 minutes

BANANA SPLIT MINI CUPCAKES

80g (2.8oz) butter, softened
½ cup brown sugar
1 egg
1 cup self-raising flour, sifted
⅓ cup milk
½ teaspoon vanilla extract
Topping
80g (2.8oz) butter, softened
½ teaspoon yellow colouring
1 cup icing (confectioner's) sugar
2 bananas, sliced, to decorate
grated chocolate, to decorate

1   Preheat the oven to 160°C (320°F). Line a 24 mini cupcake pan with mini cupcake papers. In a medium-sized bowl, use an electric mixer on high speed to cream the butter and sugar until light and fluffy. Add the egg and mix well.

2   Add the flour, milk and vanilla, and beat with an electric mixer on medium until well combined.

3   Divide the mixture evenly between the 24 mini cupcake papers. Bake for 10–15 minutes until well risen and firm to the touch. Allow to cool for a few minutes and then transfer to a wire rack. Allow to cool fully before icing (frosting).

Topping

1   Use an electric mixer on high speed to beat the butter and yellow colouring until light and fluffy. Gradually beat in icing (confectioner's) sugar until all combined, continue beating for 1 minute. Spread evenly over each cupcake and decorate with sliced bananas and grated chocolate.

Makes 24 · Preparation 20 minutes · Cooking 15 minutes

Magic stars mini cupcakes

80g (2.8oz) butter, softened
½ cup caster (berry) sugar
1 egg
1 tablespoon cocoa powder, sifted
1 cup self-raising flour, sifted
⅓ cup milk
½ teaspoon vanilla extract
Topping
80g (2.8oz) butter, softened
½ teaspoon purple colouring
1 cup icing (confectioner's) sugar
multi coloured star-shaped sprinkles to decorate

1   Preheat the oven to 160°C (320°F). Line a 24 mini cupcake pan with mini cupcake papers. In a medium-sized bowl, use an electric mixer on high speed to cream the butter and sugar until light and fluffy. Add the egg and mix well.

2   Add the cocoa, flour, milk and vanilla, and beat with an electric mixer on medium until well combined.

3   Divide the mixture evenly between the 24 mini cupcake papers. Bake for 10–15 minutes until well risen and firm to the touch. Allow to cool for a few minutes and then transfer to a wire rack. Allow to cool fully before icing (frosting).

Topping

1   Use an electric mixer on high speed to beat the butter and purple colouring until light and fluffy. Gradually beat in icing (confectioner's) sugar until all combined, continue beating for 1 minute. Place mixture into a piping bag with a star nozzle and pipe onto cupcakes. Decorate with the star-shaped sprinkles.

Makes 24 · Preparation 20 minutes · Cooking 15 minutes

Malted milk mini cupcakes

80g (2.8oz) butter, softened
½ cup caster (berry) sugar
1 egg
1 tablespoon cocoa powder, sifted
1 cup self-raising flour, sifted
⅓ cup milk
½ teaspoon vanilla extract
Topping
80g (2.8oz) butter, softened
2 tablespoons malted milk powder
1 cup icing (confectioner's) sugar
24 chocolate-covered malt balls

1   Preheat the oven to 160°C (320°F). Line a 24 mini cupcake pan with mini cupcake papers. In a medium-sized bowl, use an electric mixer on high speed to cream the butter and sugar until light and fluffy. Add the egg and mix well.

2   Add the cocoa, flour, milk and vanilla, and beat with an electric mixer on medium until well combined.

3   Divide the mixture evenly between the 24 mini cupcake papers. Bake for 10–15 minutes until well risen and firm to the touch. Allow to cool for a few minutes and then transfer to a wire rack. Allow to cool fully before icing (frosting).

Topping

1   Use an electric mixer on high speed to beat the butter and malted milk powder until light and fluffy. Gradually beat in icing (confectioner's) sugar until all combined, continue beating for 1 minute. Place mixture into a piping bag with a plain nozzle and pipe onto cupcakes. Decorate with chocolate malt balls.

Makes 24 · Preparation 20 minutes · Cooking 15 minutes

ABCS MINI CUPCAKES

80g (2.8oz) butter, softened
½ cup caster (berry) sugar
1 egg
1 cup self-raising flour, sifted
⅓ cup milk
½ teaspoon vanilla extract
½ cup sultanas (golden raisins)
Topping
1½ cups icing (confectioner's) sugar
2 tablespoons hot water
blue, red and yellow food colouring
½ cup milk chocolate, melted

1 Preheat the oven to 160°C (320°F). Line a 24 mini cupcake pan with mini cupcake papers. In a medium-sized bowl, use an electric mixer on high speed to cream the butter and sugar until light and fluffy. Add the egg and mix well.

2 Add the flour, milk, vanilla and sultanas (golden raisins), and beat with an electric mixer on medium until well combined.

3 Divide the mixture evenly between the 24 mini cupcake papers. Bake for 10–15 minutes until well risen and firm to the touch. Allow to cool for a few minutes and then transfer to a wire rack. Allow to cool fully before icing (frosting).

Topping

1 Mix the icing (confectioner's) sugar with enough hot water to make a smooth and spreadable consistency. Divide the mixture evenly between 3 bowls and tint each with a different colour. Spread the yellow icing onto 8 of the cupcakes, red onto 8 and blue on the remaining 8. Spoon the melted chocolate into a piping bag fitted with a small, plain nozzle and pipe letters of the alphabet onto each cupcake.

Makes 24 · Preparation 20 minutes · Cooking 15 minutes

Frogs mini cupcakes

80g (2.8oz) butter, softened
½ cup brown sugar
1 egg
1 tablespoon cocoa powder, sifted
1 cup self-raising flour, sifted
⅓ cup milk
½ teaspoon vanilla extract
Topping
80g (2.8oz) butter, softened
1 cup icing (confectioner's) sugar
few drops green food colouring
24 confectionary frogs

1   Preheat the oven to 160°C (320°F). Line a 24 mini cupcake pan with mini cupcake papers. In a medium-sized bowl, use an electric mixer on high speed to cream the butter and sugar until light and fluffy. Add the egg and mix well.

2   Add the cocoa, flour, milk and vanilla, and beat with an electric mixer on medium until well combined.

3   Divide the mixture evenly between the 24 mini cupcake papers. Bake for 10–15 minutes until well risen and firm to the touch. Allow to cool for a few minutes and then transfer to a wire rack. Allow to cool fully before icing (frosting).

Topping

1   Use an electric mixer on high speed to beat the butter until light and fluffy. Gradually beat in icing (confectioner's) sugar until all combined, add the green colouring and continue beating for 1 minute. Spread evenly over each cupcake. Decorate with confectionary frogs.

Makes 24 · Preparation 20 minutes · Cooking 15 minutes

STRAWBERRIES AND CREAM MINI CUPCAKES

80g (2.8oz) butter, softened
½ cup caster (berry) sugar
1 egg
1 cup self-raising flour, sifted
⅓ cup milk
½ teaspoon vanilla extract
½ cup chopped fresh strawberries
Topping
80g (2.8oz) butter, softened
1 cup icing (confectioner's) sugar
few drops pink food colouring
24 confectionary strawberries and cream

1   Preheat the oven to 160°C (320°F). Line a 24 mini cupcake pan with mini cupcake papers. In a medium-sized bowl, use an electric mixer on high speed to cream the butter and sugar until light and fluffy. Add the egg and mix well.

2   Add the flour, milk and vanilla, and beat with an electric mixer on medium until well combined. Stir in strawberries.

3   Divide the mixture evenly between the 24 mini cupcake papers. Bake for 10–15 minutes until well risen and firm to the touch. Allow to cool for a few minutes and then transfer to a wire rack. Allow to cool fully before icing (frosting).

Topping

1   Use an electric mixer on high speed to beat the butter until light and fluffy. Gradually beat in icing (confectioner's) sugar until all combined, add the pink colouring and continue beating for 1 minute. Spread evenly over each cupcake, decorate with confectionary strawberries and cream.

Makes 24 • Preparation 20 minutes • Cooking 15 minutes

FAVOURITE MINI
CUPCAKES

FAVOURITE MINI CUPCAKES

These small mouthful cupcakes are great for easy entertaining. These little treats travel easily and with the addition of special tasty toppings they are great as a quick snack at any time, be it play lunch for the children or that quick afternoon tea.

Vanilla and raspberry mini cupcakes

80g (2.8oz) butter, softened
½ cup caster (berry) sugar
1 egg
1 cup self-raising flour, sifted
⅓ cup milk
½ teaspoon vanilla extract
½ cup fresh raspberries, crushed with a fork
Topping
80g (2.8oz) butter, softened
1 teaspoon vanilla extract
1 cup icing (confectioner's) sugar
24 fresh raspberries, to decorate

1   Preheat the oven to 160°C (320°F). Line a 24 mini cupcake pan with mini cupcake papers. In a medium-sized bowl, use an electric mixer on high speed to cream the butter and sugar until light and fluffy. Add the egg and mix well.

2   Add the flour, milk and vanilla, and beat with an electric mixer on medium until well combined. Stir through raspberries.

3   Divide the mixture evenly between the 24 mini cupcake papers. Bake for 10–15 minutes until well risen and firm to the touch. Allow to cool for a few minutes and then transfer to a wire rack. Allow to cool fully before icing (frosting).

Topping

1   Use an electric mixer on high speed to beat the butter and vanilla until light and fluffy. Gradually beat in icing (confectioner's) sugar until all combined, continue beating for 1 minute. Spread evenly over each cupcake and decorate with raspberries.

Makes 24 · Preparation 20 minutes · Cooking 15 minutes

Lemon cheesecake mini cupcakes

80g (2.8oz) butter, softened
½ cup caster (berry) sugar
1 egg
1 cup self-raising flour, sifted
⅓ cup lemon curd (lemon butter)
1 teaspoon lemon zest, finely grated
Topping
⅓ cup cream cheese, softened
1 teaspoon lemon zest
1 cup icing (confectioner's) sugar
lemon curd (lemon butter), to decorate

1   Preheat the oven to 160°C (320°F). Line a 24 mini cupcake pan with mini cupcake papers. In a medium-sized bowl, use an electric mixer on high speed to cream the butter and sugar until light and fluffy. Add the egg and mix well.

2   Add the flour, lemon curd (lemon butter) and zest, and beat with an electric mixer on medium until well combined.

3   Divide the mixture evenly between the 24 mini cupcake papers. Bake for 10–15 minutes until well risen and firm to the touch. Allow to cool for a few minutes and then transfer to a wire rack. Allow to cool fully before icing (frosting).

Topping

1   Use an electric mixer on high speed to beat the cream cheese and lemon zest until light and fluffy. Gradually beat in icing (confectioner's) sugar until all combined, then continue beating for 1 minute. Spread evenly over each cupcake and decorate with a small amount of lemon curd.

Makes 24 · Preparation 20 minutes · Cooking 15 minutes

TOASTED MARSHMALLOW MINI CUPCAKES

80g (2.8oz) butter, softened
½ cup caster (berry) sugar
1 egg
1 cup self-raising flour, sifted
⅓ cup milk
½ teaspoon vanilla extract
Topping
80g (2.8oz) butter, softened
1 cup icing (confectioner's) sugar
¼ cup mini marshmallows
toasted coconut, to decorate

1   Preheat the oven to 160°C (320°F). Line a 24 mini cupcake pan with mini cupcake papers. In a medium-sized bowl, use an electric mixer on high speed to cream the butter and sugar until light and fluffy. Add the egg and mix well.

2   Add the flour, milk and vanilla, and beat with an electric mixer on medium until well combined.

3   Divide the mixture evenly between the 24 mini cupcake papers. Bake for 10–15 minutes until well risen and firm to the touch. Allow to cool for a few minutes and then transfer to a wire rack. Allow to cool fully before icing (frosting).

Topping

1   Use an electric mixer on high speed to beat the butter until light and fluffy. Gradually beat in icing (confectioner's) sugar until all combined, continue beating for 1 minute, stir though mini marshmallows. Spread evenly over each cupcake and decorate with toasted coconut.

Makes 24 · Preparation 20 minutes · Cooking 15 minutes

VALENTINES MINI CUPCAKES

80g (2.8oz) butter, softened
½ cup caster (berry) sugar
1 egg
1 cup self-raising flour, sifted
¼ cup milk
½ teaspoon pink food colouring
Topping
1 cup white chocolate buttons
¼ cup cream
mini heart sprinkles, to decorate

1   Preheat the oven to 160°C (320°F). Line a 24 mini cupcake pan with mini cupcake papers. In a medium-sized bowl, use an electric mixer on high speed to cream the butter and sugar until light and fluffy. Add the egg and mix well.

2   Add the flour, milk and pink colouring, and beat with an electric mixer on medium until well combined.

3   Divide the mixture evenly between the 24 mini cupcake papers. Bake for 10–15 minutes until well risen and firm to the touch. Allow to cool for a few minutes and then transfer to a wire rack. Allow to cool fully before icing (frosting).

Topping

1   Melt the white chocolate and cream together in a heatproof bowl over a saucepan of boiling water. Allow to cool and thicken. Spoon mixture into a piping bag fitted with a large plain nozzle and pipe onto cupcakes. Decorate with heart sprinkles.

Makes 24 · Preparation 20 minutes · Cooking 15 minutes

CHRISTMAS TREE MINI CUPCAKES

80g (2.8oz) butter, softened
½ cup caster (berry) sugar
1 egg
1 cup self-raising flour, sifted
1 tablespoon cocoa powder, sifted
⅓ cup milk
½ teaspoon vanilla extract
Topping
80g (2.8oz) butter, softened
1 cup icing (confectioner's) sugar
green food colouring
white edible glitter to decorate

1 Preheat the oven to 160°C (320°F). Line a 24 mini cupcake pan with mini cupcake papers. In a medium-sized bowl, use an electric mixer on high speed to cream the butter and sugar until light and fluffy. Add the egg and mix well.

2 Add the flour, cocoa, milk and vanilla, and beat with an electric mixer on medium until well combined.

3 Divide the mixture evenly between the 24 mini cupcake papers. Bake for 10–15 minutes until well risen and firm to the touch. Allow to cool for a few minutes and then transfer to a wire rack. Allow to cool fully before icing (frosting).

Topping

1 Use an electric mixer on high speed to beat the butter until light and fluffy. Gradually beat in icing (confectioner's) sugar until all combined, add green colouring and continue beating for 1 minute. Spoon mixture into a piping bag fitted with a large star nozzle and pipe onto cupcakes to form a point. Sprinkle with edible glitter.

Makes 24 · Preparation 20 minutes · Cooking 15 minutes

EASTER MINI CUPCAKES

80g (2.8oz) butter, softened
½ cup caster (berry) sugar
1 egg
1 cup self-raising flour, sifted
⅓ cup milk
½ teaspoon vanilla extract
½ cup choc chips
Topping
80g (2.8oz) butter, softened
1 cup icing (confectioner's) sugar
1 tablespoon cocoa powder, sifted
mini Easter eggs, to decorate

1   Preheat the oven to 160°C (320°F). Line a 24 mini cupcake pan with mini cupcake papers. In a medium-sized bowl, use an electric mixer on high speed to cream the butter and sugar until light and fluffy. Add the egg and mix well.

2   Add the flour, milk and vanilla, and beat with an electric mixer on medium until well combined, stir through choc chips.

3   Divide the mixture evenly between the 24 mini cupcake papers. Bake for 10–15 minutes until well risen and firm to the touch. Allow to cool for a few minutes and then transfer to a wire rack. Allow to cool fully before icing (frosting).

Topping

1   Use an electric mixer on high speed to beat the butter until light and fluffy. Gradually beat in icing (confectioner's) sugar and cocoa until all combined, then continue beating for 1 minute. Spread evenly over each cupcake and decorate with mini Easter eggs.

Makes 24 • Preparation 20 minutes • Cooking 15 minutes

COCONUT ICE MINI CUPCAKES

80g (2.8oz) butter, softened
½ cup caster (berry) sugar
1 egg
1 cup self-raising flour, sifted
⅓ cup coconut milk
½ teaspoon vanilla extract
½ cup desiccated (fine) coconut
Topping
1½ cups icing (confectioner's) sugar
2 tablespoons hot water
few drops pink food colouring
¼ cup desiccated (fine) coconut

1   Preheat the oven to 160°C(320°F). Line a 24 mini cupcake pan with mini cupcake papers. In a medium-sized bowl, use an electric mixer on high speed to cream the butter and sugar until light and fluffy. Add the egg and mix well.

2   Add the flour, coconut milk and vanilla, and beat with an electric mixer on medium until well combined. Stir through desiccated (fine) coconut.

3   Divide the mixture evenly between the 24 mini cupcake papers. Bake for 10–15 minutes until well risen and firm to the touch. Allow to cool for a few minutes and then transfer to a wire rack. Allow to cool fully before icing (frosting).

Topping

1   Mix icing (confectioner's) sugar with enough hot water to make a smooth paste, tint pink with colouring and stir through desiccated coconut. Spread evenly over each cupcake.

Makes 24 · Preparation 20 minutes · Cooking 15 minutes

QUICK & EASY
MINI CUPCAKES

QUICK & EASY MINI CUPCAKES

In all of baking there is nothing easier than producing a plate of warm enticing cupcakes. The batter is so easy to make it almost makes itself and you can use any sugar- or cream-based topping you fancy. Also purchase a selection of novelty cake decorations to have on hand to assist your creative designs.

STRAWBERRY MINI CUPCAKES

80g (2.8oz) butter, softened
½ cup caster (berry) sugar
1 egg
1 cup self-raising flour, sifted
⅓ cup milk
½ teaspoon vanilla extract
½ cup fresh strawberries, chopped
Topping
1½ cups icing (confectioner's) sugar
2 tablespoons hot water
few drops pink colouring
strawberries, sliced, to decorate

1   Preheat the oven to 160°C (320°F). Line a 24 mini cupcake pan with mini cupcake papers. In a medium-sized bowl, use an electric mixer on high speed to cream the butter and sugar until light and fluffy. Add the egg and mix well.

2   Add the flour, milk and vanilla, and beat with an electric mixer on medium until well combined, then stir through chopped strawberries.

3   Divide the mixture evenly between the 24 mini cupcake papers. Bake for 10–15 minutes until well risen and firm to the touch. Allow to cool for a few minutes and then transfer to a wire rack. Allow to cool fully before icing (frosting).

Topping

1   Mix the icing (confectioner's) sugar with enough hot water to make a smooth paste, and tint pink with a few drops of colouring. Spread evenly over each cupcake and decorate with sliced strawberries.

Makes 24 · Preparation 20 minutes · Cooking 15 minutes

Lemon mini cupcakes

80g (2.8oz) butter, softened
½ cup caster (berry) sugar
1 egg
1 cup self-raising flour, sifted
⅓ cup milk
1 teaspoon lemon zest, finely grated
Topping
1½ cups icing (confectioner's) sugar
2 tablespoons lemon juice

1   Preheat the oven to 160°C (320°F). Line a 24 mini cupcake pan with mini cupcake papers. In a medium-sized bowl, use an electric mixer on high speed to cream the butter and sugar until light and fluffy. Add the egg and mix well.

2   Add the flour, milk and zest, and beat with an electric mixer on medium until well combined.

3   Divide the mixture evenly between the 24 mini cupcake papers. Bake for 10–15 minutes until well risen and firm to the touch. Allow to cool for a few minutes and then transfer to a wire rack. Allow to cool fully before icing (frosting).

Topping

1   Mix the icing (confectioner's) sugar with enough lemon juice to form a smooth paste. Spread evenly over each cupcake.

Makes 24 · Preparation 20 minutes · Cooking 15 minutes

COFFEE AND PECAN MINI CUPCAKES

80g (2.8oz) butter, softened
½ cup caster (berry) sugar
1 egg
1 cup self-raising flour, sifted
⅓ cup milk
½ teaspoon vanilla extract
½ cup pecans, chopped
Topping
80g (2.8oz) butter, softened
1 teaspoon instant coffee powder
1 cup icing (confectioner's) sugar
pecans, chopped, to decorate

1   Preheat the oven to 160°C (320°F). Line a 24 mini cupcake pan with mini cupcake papers. In a medium-sized bowl, use an electric mixer on high speed to cream the butter and sugar until light and fluffy. Add the egg and mix well.

2   Add the flour, milk and vanilla, and beat with an electric mixer on medium until well combined. Stir through pecans.

3   Divide the mixture evenly between the 24 mini cupcake papers. Bake for 10–15 minutes until well risen and firm to the touch. Allow to cool for a few minutes and then transfer to a wire rack. Allow to cool fully before icing (frosting).

Topping

1   Use an electric mixer on high speed to beat the butter and coffee until light and fluffy. Gradually beat in icing (confectioner's) sugar until all combined, then continue beating for 1 minute. Spoon mixture into a piping bag fitted with a large star nozzle and pipe onto cupcakes, and decorate with chopped pecans.

Makes 24 · Preparation 20 minutes · Cooking 15 minutes

Vanilla mini cupcakes

80g (2.8oz) butter, softened
½ cup caster (berry) sugar
1 egg
1 cup self-raising flour, sifted
⅓ cup milk
½ teaspoon vanilla extract
Topping
80g (2.8oz) butter, softened
1 teaspoon vanilla extract
1 cup icing (confectioner's) sugar

1   Preheat the oven to 160°C (320°F). Line a 24 mini cupcake pan with mini cupcake papers. In a medium-sized bowl, use an electric mixer on high speed to cream the butter and sugar until light and fluffy. Add the egg and mix well.
2   Add the flour, milk and vanilla, and beat with an electric mixer on medium until well combined.
3   Divide the mixture evenly between the 24 mini cupcake papers. Bake for 10–15 minutes until well risen and firm to the touch. Allow to cool for a few minutes and then transfer to a wire rack. Allow to cool fully before icing (frosting).

Topping

1   Use an electric mixer on high speed to beat the butter and vanilla until light and fluffy. Gradually beat in icing (confectioner's) sugar until all combined, then continue beating for 1 minute. Spoon mixture into a piping bag fitted with a large star nozzle and pipe onto cupcakes.

Makes 24 · Preparation 20 minutes · Cooking 15 minutes

LEMON MERINGUE MINI CUPCAKES

80g (2.8oz) butter, softened
½ cup caster (berry) sugar
1 egg
1 cup self-raising flour, sifted
⅓ cup milk
1 teaspoon lemon zest, finely grated
Topping
1 cup lemon curd (lemon butter)
24 mini meringue decorations

1   Preheat the oven to 160°C (320°F). Line a 24 mini cupcake pan with mini cupcake papers. In a medium-sized bowl, use an electric mixer on high speed to cream the butter and sugar until light and fluffy. Add the egg and mix well.

2   Add the flour, milk and zest, and beat with an electric mixer on medium until well combined.

3   Divide the mixture evenly between the 24 mini cupcake papers. Bake for 10–15 minutes until well risen and firm to the touch. Allow to cool for a few minutes and then transfer to a wire rack. Allow to cool fully before icing (frosting).

Topping

1   Top each cupcake with a teaspoon of lemon curd (lemon butter) and a mini meringue.

Makes 24 • Preparation 20 minutes • Cooking 15 minutes

COCONUT AND LIME MINI CUPCAKES

80g (2.8oz) butter, softened
½ cup caster (berry) sugar
1 egg
1 cup self-raising flour, sifted
⅓ cup milk
1 teaspoon lime zest, finely grated
½ cup desiccated (fine) coconut
Topping
1 cup icing (confectioner's) sugar
1 teaspoon lime zest, finely grated
2 tablespoons lime juice
green food colouring
desiccated (fine) coconut, to decorate

1 Preheat the oven to 160°C (320°F). Line a 24 mini cupcake pan with mini cupcake papers. In a medium-sized bowl, use an electric mixer on high speed to cream the butter and sugar until light and fluffy. Add the egg and mix well.

2 Add the flour, milk and zest, and beat with an electric mixer on medium until well combined. Stir through coconut.

3 Divide the mixture evenly between the 24 mini cupcake papers. Bake for 10–15 minutes until well risen and firm to the touch. Allow to cool for a few minutes and then transfer to a wire rack. Allow to cool fully before icing (frosting).

Topping

1 Mix icing (confectioner's) sugar and lime zest with enough lime juice to make a smooth paste, tint light green. Spread evenly over each cupcake. Decorate with desiccated (fine) coconut.

Makes 24 · Preparation 20 minutes · Cooking 15 minutes

QUICK CHOCOLATE MINI CUPCAKES

80g (2.8oz) butter, softened
½ cup caster (berry) sugar
1 egg
1 cup self-raising flour, sifted
2 tablespoon cocoa, sifted
⅓ cup milk
½ teaspoon vanilla extract
Topping
¼ cup cream
1 cup dark chocolate buttons

1   Preheat the oven to 160°C (320°F). Line a 24 mini cupcake pan with mini cupcake papers. In a medium-sized bowl, use an electric mixer on high speed to cream the butter and sugar until light and fluffy. Add the egg and mix well.

2   Add the flour, cocoa, milk and vanilla, and beat with an electric mixer on medium until well combined.

3   Divide the mixture evenly between the 24 mini cupcake papers. Bake for 10–15 minutes until well risen and firm to the touch. Allow to cool for a few minutes and then transfer to a wire rack. Allow to cool fully before icing (frosting).

Topping

1   Combine the cream and chocolate buttons in a heatproof bowl over a saucepan of boiling water and stir until melted. Allow to cool and thicken. Spread evenly over cupcakes.

Makes 24 · Preparation 20 minutes · Cooking 15 minutes

SUGAR AND SPICE MINI CUPCAKES

80g (2.8oz) butter, softened
½ cup caster (berry) sugar
1 egg
1 cup self-raising flour, sifted
⅓ cup milk
1 teaspoon mixed spice
Topping
80g (2.8oz) butter, softened
1 cup icing (confectioner's) sugar
mixed spice

1   Preheat the oven to 160°C (320°F). Line a 24 mini cupcake pan with mini cupcake papers. In a medium-sized bowl, use an electric mixer on high speed to cream the butter and sugar until light and fluffy. Add the egg and mix well.

2   Add the flour, milk and spice, and beat with an electric mixer on medium until well combined.

3   Divide the mixture evenly between the 24 mini cupcake papers. Bake for 10–15 minutes until well risen and firm to the touch. Allow to cool for a few minutes and then transfer to a wire rack. Allow to cool fully before icing (frosting).

Topping

1   Use an electric mixer on high speed to beat the butter until light and fluffy. Gradually beat in icing (confectioner's) sugar until all combined, continue beating for 1 minute. Spoon mixture into a piping bag fitted with a large plain nozzle and pipe onto cupcakes, dust lightly with mixed spice.

Makes 24 · Preparation 20 minutes · Cooking 15 minutes

CHOCOLATE
CUPCAKES

CHOCOLATE CUPCAKES

This set of recipes will give you a whole new collection of ways to create chocolate cupcake favourites for the whole family, or for that special evening or weekend of indulgence.

LEMON GANACHE CUPCAKES

2 eggs
125g (4.4oz) butter, softened
1 cup caster (berry) sugar
½ cup milk
2 cups self-raising flour, sifted
1 teaspoon vanilla extract
100g (3.5oz) dark (semi-sweet) chocolate pieces
1 tablespoon cocoa powder
1 teaspoon lemon extract
Topping
100g (3.5oz) dark (semi-sweet) chocolate, grated
20g (0.7oz) butter, softened
⅓ cup thickened (whipping) cream
1 teaspoon lemon extract
1 piece crystallised (candied) lemon, cut into slivers

1   Preheat the oven to 160°C (320°F). Line a 12-cupcake pan with cupcake papers. In a medium-sized bowl, lightly beat the eggs, add butter and sugar, then mix until light and fluffy.

2   Add milk, flour and vanilla, and stir to combine. Add remaining ingredients. Beat with an electric mixer for 2 minutes, until light and creamy.

3   Divide the mixture evenly between the cake papers. Bake for 18–20 minutes until risen and firm to touch. Allow to cool for a few minutes and then transfer to a wire rack. Allow to cool fully before icing (frosting).

Topping

1   Meanwhile, combine the chocolate and butter in a medium-sized saucepan over a medium heat. As the mixture begins to melt, reduce heat to low, stirring constantly, until melted. Remove from heat, add cream and lemon extract, and stir. Rest for 10 minutes: the mixture will be firm and velvety in consistency.

2   Once cool, put in a piping bag with a small plain nozzle. Pipe topping onto cupcakes in a spiral and top with crystallised (candied) lemon pieces.

Makes 12 · Preparation 12 minutes · Cooking 20 minutes

Double choc cupcakes

2 eggs
125g (4.4oz) butter, softened
1 cup caster (berry) sugar
½ cup milk
2 cups self-raising flour, sifted
100g (3.5oz) dark (semi-sweet) chocolate pieces
1 tablespoon cocoa powder
Topping
100g (3.5oz) white chocolate, chopped
20g (0.7oz) butter, softened
⅓ cup thickened (whipping) cream
1 teaspoon icing (confectioner's) sugar
dark (semi-sweet) chocolate, grated, to decorate

1 Preheat the oven to 160°C (320°F). Line a 12-cupcake pan with cupcake papers. In a medium-sized bowl, lightly beat the eggs, add butter and sugar, then mix until light and fluffy.

2 Add milk and flour, and stir to combine. Add the dark (semi-sweet) chocolate and cocoa powder, and stir through mixture. Beat with an electric mixer for 2 minutes, until light and creamy.

3 Divide the mixture evenly between the cake papers. Bake for 18–20 minutes until risen and firm to touch. Allow to cool for a few minutes and then transfer to a wire rack. Allow to cool fully before icing (frosting).

Topping

1 Meanwhile, combine the white chocolate and butter in a medium-sized saucepan over a medium heat. As the mixture begins to melt, reduce heat to low, stirring constantly, until melted. Remove from heat, add cream and icing (confectioner's) sugar, and stir to combine. Rest for 10 minutes: the mixture will be firm and velvety in consistency.

2 Spread icing sugar with the back of a spoon over cupcakes and decorate with grated dark chocolate.

Makes 12 · Preparation 12 minutes · Cooking 20 minutes

CHOCOLATE MALT CUPCAKES

2 eggs
125g (4.4oz) butter, softened
1 cup caster (berry) sugar
½ cup buttermilk
2 cups self-raising flour, sifted
1 teaspoon vanilla extract
¼ cup malted milk powder
2 tablespoons cocoa powder
Topping
½ cup chocolate drops
½ cup butter, softened
⅓ cup thickened (whipping) cream
1½ cups icing (confectioner's) sugar
1 teaspoon vanilla extract
½ cup chocolate malt balls, crushed

1   Preheat the oven to 160°C (320°F). Line a 12-cupcake pan with cupcake papers. In a medium-sized bowl, lightly beat the eggs, add butter and sugar, then mix until light and fluffy.

2   Add buttermilk, flour, vanilla, malted milk powder and cocoa powder, and stir to combine. Beat with an electric mixer for 2 minutes, until light and creamy.

3   Divide the mixture evenly between the cake papers. Bake for 18–20 minutes until risen and firm to touch. Allow to cool for a few minutes and then transfer to a wire rack. Allow to cool fully before icing (frosting).

Topping

1   Meanwhile, combine the chocolate and half of the butter in a medium-sized saucepan over medium heat. As the mixture begins to melt, reduce heat to low, stirring constantly, until melted. Remove from heat, add cream, and stir. Rest for 10 minutes: the mixture will be firm and velvety in consistency.

2   Combine remaining butter, icing (confectioner's) sugar and vanilla extract, and stir until light and fluffy. Add melted chocolate mixture, and stir to combine. Apply icing to each cupcake with a knife. Top each cupcake with chocolate malt pieces.

Makes 12 · Preparation 12 minutes · Cooking 20 minutes

CHOCOLATE CUPCAKES

2 eggs
125g (4.4oz) butter, softened
1 cup caster (berry) sugar
½ cup buttermilk
2 cups self-raising flour, sifted
1 teaspoon cocoa powder
1 teaspoon vanilla extract
½ cup milk chocolate pieces, finely chopped
⅓ cup unthickened (half and half/single) cream
Topping
1½ cups icing (confectioner's) sugar
½ cup butter, softened
2 tablespoons cocoa powder
sugar (candy) flowers (available from cake decorating shops)

1 Preheat the oven to 160°C (320°F). Line a 12-cupcake pan with cupcake papers. In a medium-sized bowl, lightly beat the eggs, add butter and sugar, then mix until light and fluffy.

2 Add buttermilk, flour, cocoa powder and vanilla, and stir to combine. Beat with an electric mixer for 2 minutes, until light and creamy. Add chocolate and cream, stir mixture thoroughly.

3 Divide the mixture evenly between the cake papers. Bake for 18–20 minutes until risen and firm to touch. Allow to cool for a few minutes and then transfer to a wire rack. Allow to cool fully before icing (frosting).

Topping

1 Meanwhile, combine half the icing (confectioner's) sugar and butter, mix with a wooden spoon, add remaining icing sugar, butter and cocoa and beat with the spoon until light and fluffy.

2 Add icing to a piping bag and pipe onto cupcakes, then smooth over with spatula and top with flower decorations.

Makes 12 · Preparation 15 minutes · Cooking 20 minutes

WHITE CHOC CHIP CUPCAKES

2 eggs
125g (4.4oz) butter, softened
1 cup caster (berry) sugar
½ cup milk
2 cups self-raising flour, sifted
1 teaspoon vanilla extract
½ cup white chocolate drops
1 tablespoon cocoa powder
Topping
½ cup milk chocolate, grated
½ cup butter, softened
⅓ cup thickened (whipping) cream
1½ cups icing (confectioner's) sugar
1 teaspoon vanilla extract
½ cup white chocolate drops
½ cup white chocolate drops to decorate

1   Preheat the oven to 160°C (320°F). Line a 12-cupcake pan with cupcake papers. In a medium-sized bowl, lightly beat the eggs, add butter and sugar, then mix until light and fluffy.

2   Beat with an electric mixer for 2 minutes, until light and creamy. Add milk, flour and vanilla, and stir to combine. Add white chocolate and cocoa powder and stir through mixture.

3   Divide the mixture evenly between the cake papers. Bake for 18–20 minutes until risen and firm to touch. Allow to cool for a few minutes and then transfer to a wire rack. Allow to cool fully before icing (frosting).

Topping

1   Meanwhile, combine the milk chocolate and half of the butter in a medium-sized saucepan over a medium heat. As the mixture begins to melt, reduce heat to low, stirring constantly, until melted. Remove from heat, add cream and stir. Rest for 10 minutes: the mixture will be firm and velvety in consistency.

2   Combine remaining butter, icing (confectioner's) sugar and vanilla extract, and stir until light and fluffy. Add melted chocolate mixture, stir in chocolate drops and spoon onto cupcakes. Sprinkle with chocolate drops.

Makes 12 • Preparation 20 minutes • Cooking 20 minutes

DARK CHOC TRUFFLE CUPCAKES

2 eggs
125g (4.4oz) butter, softened
1 cup caster (berry) sugar
½ cup vanilla-flavoured yoghurt
2 cups self-raising flour, sifted
1 tablespoon vanilla extract
100g (3.5oz) dark (semi-sweet) chocolate pieces
1 tablespoon cocoa powder
Topping
100g (3.5oz) dark (semi-sweet) chocolate pieces
20g (0.7oz) butter, softened
⅓ cup thickened (whipping) cream
cocoa powder for dusting

1   Preheat the oven to 160°C (320°F). Line a 12-cupcake pan with cupcake papers. In a medium-sized bowl, lightly beat the eggs, add butter and sugar, then mix until light and fluffy.

2   Add yoghurt, flour and vanilla, and stir to combine. Add remaining ingredients. Beat with an electric mixer for 2 minutes, until light and creamy.

3   Divide the mixture evenly between the cake papers. Bake for 18–20 minutes until risen and firm to touch. Allow to cool for a few minutes, and then transfer to a wire rack. Allow to cool fully before icing (frosting).

Topping

1   Meanwhile, combine the chocolate and butter in a medium-sized saucepan over a medium heat. As the mixture begins to melt, reduce heat to low, stirring constantly, until melted. Remove from heat, add cream and stir. Rest for 10 minutes: the mixture will be firm and velvety in consistency.

2   Use a piping bag fitted with a star nozzle to pipe the mixture onto the cupcakes. Dust heavily with cocoa powder.

Makes 12 • Preparation 12 minutes • Cooking 20 minutes

CHILLI SPICE CUPCAKES

2 small fresh chillies or 1 teaspoon dry red chilli flakes
2 eggs
125g (4.4oz) butter, softened
1 cup caster (berry) sugar
½ cup milk
2 cups self-raising flour, sifted
1 teaspoon vanilla extract
100g (3.5oz) dark (semi-sweet) chocolate pieces
1 tablespoon cocoa powder
1 teaspoon cinnamon
⅛ cup chilli-infused water
Topping
100g (3.5oz) dark (semi-sweet) chocolate, chopped
20g (0.7oz) butter, softened
⅓ cup thickened (whipping) cream
⅛ cup chilli-infused water
cinnamon for dusting

1   Preheat the oven to 160°C (320°F). Line a 12-cupcake pan with cupcake papers. Slice chillies down the centre and remove seeds – place the chillies in a cup with ¼ cup of hot water to soak for 10 minutes. In a medium-sized bowl, lightly beat the eggs, add butter and sugar, then mix until light and fluffy.

2   Add milk, flour and vanilla, and stir to combine. Add the chocolate, cocoa powder, cinnamon and half the chilli-infused water, and combine. Beat with an electric mixer for 2 minutes, until light and creamy.

3   Divide the mixture evenly between the cake papers. Bake for 18–20 minutes until risen and firm to touch. Allow to cool for a few minutes and then transfer to a wire rack. Allow to cool fully before icing (frosting).

Topping

1   Meanwhile, combine the chocolate and butter in a medium-sized saucepan over a medium heat. As the mixture begins to melt, reduce heat to low, stirring constantly until melted. Remove from heat, add cream and remaining chilli water and stir. Rest for 10 minutes: the mixture will be firm and velvety in consistency.

2   Put in a piping bag with a small plain nozzle and pipe onto cakes. Dust with cinnamon.

Makes 12 · Preparation 12 minutes · Cooking 20 minutes

MACADAMIA CHOC CUPCAKES

3 eggs
125g (4.4oz) butter, softened
1 cup caster (berry) sugar
½ cup milk
1½ cups self-raising flour, sifted
1 teaspoon vanilla extract
1 tablespoon cocoa powder
¼ cup chopped macadamias

Topping
½ cup caster (berry) sugar, for toffee
100g (3.5oz) dark (semi-sweet) chocolate
20g (0.7oz) butter, softened
⅓ cup thickened (whipping) cream
1 cup icing (confectioner's) sugar
1 tablespoon cocoa powder
100g chopped macadamias

1   Preheat the oven to 160°C (320°F). Line a 12-cupcake pan with cupcake papers. In a medium-sized bowl, lightly beat the eggs, add butter and sugar, then mix until light and fluffy.

2   Add milk, flour, vanilla and cocoa powder, and stir to combine. Beat with an electric mixer for 2 minutes, until light and creamy, then stir in macadamias.

3   Divide the mixture evenly between the cake papers. Bake for 18–20 minutes until risen and firm to touch. Allow to cool for a few minutes and then transfer to a wire rack. Allow to cool fully before icing (frosting).

Toffee

1   Place caster (berry) sugar evenly on a greaseproof paper–lined baking tray, and bake at 200°C (400°F) for approximately 25 minutes until toffee consistency forms. Cool until hardened.

Topping

1   Combine the chocolate and butter in a medium-sized saucepan over a medium heat. As the mixture begins to melt, reduce heat to low, stirring constantly, until melted. Remove from heat, add cream and stir. Rest for 10 minutes: the mixture will be firm and velvety in consistency.

2   Combine the icing (confectioner's) sugar and cocoa powder. Add the chocolate mixture and mix with a wooden spoon until light and fluffy. Spread evenly onto the cupcakes with a teaspoon or spatula. Decorate with macadamia and broken toffee pieces.

Makes 12 · Preparation 12 minutes · Cooking 45 minutes

MOCHA MINI CUPCAKES

80g (2.8oz) butter, softened
½ cup caster (berry) sugar
1 egg
1 cup self-raising flour, sifted
1 tablespoon cocoa, sifted
⅓ cup milk
1 teaspoon instant coffee
Topping
80g (2.8oz) butter, softened
1 teaspoon instant coffee
1 cup icing (confectioner's) sugar
dark (semi-sweet) chocolate, grated, to decorate

1   Preheat the oven to 160°C (320°F). Line a 24 mini cupcake pan with mini cupcake papers. In a medium-sized bowl, use an electric mixer on high speed to cream the butter and sugar until light and fluffy. Add the egg and mix well.

2   Add the flour, cocoa, milk and coffee, and beat with an electric mixer on medium until well combined.

3   Divide the mixture evenly between the 24 mini cupcake papers. Bake for 10–15 minutes until well risen and firm to the touch. Allow to cool for a few minutes and then transfer to a wire rack. Allow to cool fully before icing (frosting).

Topping

1   Use an electric mixer on high speed to beat the butter and coffee until light and fluffy. Gradually beat in icing (confectioner's) sugar until all combined, continue beating for 1 minute.

2   Spoon mixture into a piping bag fitted with a large star nozzle and pipe onto cupcakes, decorate with grated chocolate.

Makes 24 · Preparation 20 minutes · Cooking 15 minutes

CHOC-MINT CRISP MINI CUPCAKES

80g (2.8oz) butter, softened
½ cup caster (berry) sugar
1 egg
1 cup self-raising flour, sifted
1 tablespoon cocoa, sifted
⅓ cup milk
½ teaspoon peppermint extract
Topping
1 cup milk chocolate drops
¼ cup cream
peppermint crisp confectionary, crushed

1   Preheat the oven to 160°C (320°F). Line a 24 mini cupcake pan with mini cupcake papers. In a medium-sized bowl, use an electric mixer on high speed to cream the butter and sugar until light and fluffy. Add the egg and mix well.

2   Add the flour, cocoa, milk and peppermint extract, and beat with an electric mixer on medium until well combined.

3   Divide the mixture evenly between the 24 mini cupcake papers. Bake for 10–15 minutes until well risen and firm to the touch. Allow to cool for a few minutes and then transfer to a wire rack. Allow to cool fully before icing (frosting).

Topping

1   Combine the chocolate and cream in a heatproof bowl over a saucepan of boiling water and stir until melted. Allow to cool and thicken, then spread over the cupcakes. Decorate with peppermint crisp.

Makes 24 · Preparation 20 minutes · Cooking 15 minutes

WHITE CHOCOLATE MINI CUPCAKES

80g (2.8oz) butter, softened
½ cup caster (berry) sugar
1 egg
1 cup self-raising flour, sifted
⅓ cup milk
½ teaspoon vanilla extract
½ cup white chocolate chips
Topping
1 cup white chocolate drops
¼ cup cream
white chocolate, grated, to decorate

1. Preheat the oven to 160°C (320°F). Line a 24 mini cupcake pan with mini cupcake papers. In a medium-sized bowl, use an electric mixer on high speed to cream the butter and sugar until light and fluffy. Add the egg and mix well.

2. Add the flour, milk and vanilla, and beat with an electric mixer on medium until well combined. Fold through chocolate chips.

3. Divide the mixture evenly between the 24 mini cupcake papers. Bake for 10–15 minutes until well risen and firm to the touch. Allow to cool for a few minutes and then transfer to a wire rack. Allow to cool fully before icing (frosting).

Topping

1. Combine the chocolate and cream in a heatproof bowl over a saucepan of boiling water, stirring until melted. Allow to cool and thicken, then spread over cupcakes. Decorate with grated white chocolate.

Makes 24 · Preparation 20 minutes · Cooking 15 minutes

CHOCOLATE NOUGAT MINI CUPCAKES

80g (2.8oz) butter, softened
½ cup honey
1 egg
1 cup self-raising flour, sifted
1 tablespoon cocoa, sifted
⅓ cup milk
½ teaspoon vanilla extract
½ cup roasted almonds, chopped
Topping
80g (2.8oz) butter, softened
1 cup icing (confectioner's) sugar
1 tablespoon cocoa, sifted
nougat, chopped, to decorate

1   Preheat the oven to 160°C (320°F). Line a 24 mini cupcake pan with mini cupcake papers. In a medium-sized bowl, use an electric mixer on high speed to cream the butter and honey until light and fluffy. Add the egg and mix well.

2   Add the flour, cocoa, milk and vanilla, and beat with an electric mixer on medium until well combined. Fold through chopped almonds.

3   Divide the mixture evenly between the 24 mini cupcake papers. Bake for 10–15 minutes until well risen and firm to the touch. Allow to cool for a few minutes and then transfer to a wire rack. Allow to cool fully before icing (frosting).

Topping

1   Use an electric mixer on high speed to beat the butter until light and fluffy. Gradually beat in icing (confectioner's) sugar and cocoa until all combined, continue beating for 1 minute. Use a piping bag fitted with a star nozzle to pipe the icing onto the cupcakes and decorate with chopped nougat.

Makes 24 • Preparation 20 minutes • Cooking 15 minutes

CHERRY COCONUT MINI CUPCAKES

80g (2.8oz) butter, softened
½ cup caster (berry) sugar
1 egg
1 cup self-raising flour, sifted
⅓ cup milk
½ teaspoon vanilla extract
¼ cup glacé (glazed) cherries, chopped
¼ cup desiccated (fine) coconut
Topping
1 cup dark (semi-sweet) chocolate drops
¼ cup cream
glacé (glazed) cherries, to decorate
desiccated (fine) coconut, to decorate

1   Preheat the oven to 160°C (320°F). Line a 24 mini cupcake pan with mini cupcake papers. In a medium-sized bowl, use an electric mixer on high speed to cream the butter and sugar until light and fluffy. Add the egg and mix well.

2   Add the flour, milk and vanilla, and beat with an electric mixer on medium until well combined. Fold through the cherries and coconut.

3   Divide the mixture evenly between the 24 mini cupcake papers. Bake for 10–15 minutes until well risen and firm to the touch. Allow to cool for a few minutes and then transfer to a wire rack. Allow to cool fully before icing (frosting).

Topping

1   Combine the chocolate and cream in a heatproof bowl over a saucepan of boiling water, stirring until melted. Allow it to cool and thicken. Spread evenly over each cupcake. Decorate with cherries and coconut.

Makes 24 • Preparation 20 minutes • Cooking 15 minutes

CHOCOLATE AND STRAWBERRY MINI CUPCAKES

80g (2.8oz) butter, softened
½ cup caster (berry) sugar
1 egg
1 cup self-raising flour, sifted
⅓ cup milk
½ teaspoon vanilla extract
¼ cup fresh strawberries, chopped
¼ cup milk chocolate chips
Topping
80g (2.8oz) butter, softened
1 cup icing (confectioner's) sugar
1 tablespoon cocoa, sifted
fresh strawberries, sliced, to decorate

1   Preheat the oven to 160°C (320°F). Line a 24 mini cupcake pan with mini cupcake papers. In a medium-sized bowl, use an electric mixer on high speed to cream the butter and sugar until light and fluffy. Add the egg and mix well.

2   Add the flour, milk and vanilla, and beat with an electric mixer on medium until well combined. Fold through strawberries and chocolate chips.

3   Divide the mixture evenly between the 24 mini cupcake papers. Bake for 10–15 minutes until well risen and firm to the touch. Allow to cool for a few minutes and then transfer to a wire rack. Allow to cool fully before icing (frosting).

Topping

1   Use an electric mixer on high speed to beat the butter until light and fluffy. Gradually beat in icing (confectioner's) sugar and cocoa until all combined, continue beating for 1 minute. Use a piping bag fitted with a star nozzle to pipe the icing onto the cupcakes, then decorate with strawberries.

Makes 24 · Preparation 20 minutes · Cooking 15 minutes

Chocolate hazelnut mini cupcakes

80g (2.8oz) butter, softened
½ cup caster (berry) sugar
1 egg
1 cup self-raising flour, sifted
⅓ cup milk
½ teaspoon vanilla extract
¼ cup roasted hazelnuts, chopped
¼ cup dark (semi-sweet) chocolate chips
Topping
1 cup chocolate hazelnut spread
roasted hazelnuts, chopped, to decorate
dark (semi-sweet) chocolate, grated, to decorate

1   Preheat the oven to 160°C (320°F). Line a 24 mini cupcake pan with mini cupcake papers. In a medium-sized bowl, use an electric mixer on high speed to cream the butter and sugar until light and fluffy. Add the egg and mix well.

2   Add the flour, milk and vanilla, and beat with an electric mixer on medium until well combined. Fold through hazelnuts and chocolate chips.

3   Divide the mixture evenly between the 24 mini cupcake papers. Bake for 10–15 minutes until well risen and firm to the touch. Allow to cool for a few minutes and then transfer to a wire rack. Allow to cool fully before icing (frosting).

Topping

1   Spread chocolate hazelnut spread evenly over each cupcake and decorate with hazelnuts and grated chocolate.

Makes 24 · Preparation 20 minutes · Cooking 15 minutes

Choc caramel mini cupcakes

80g (2.8oz) butter, softened
½ cup caster (berry) sugar
1 egg
1 cup self-raising flour, sifted
2 tablespoons cocoa, sifted
⅓ cup milk
½ cup white chocolate chips
Topping
1 cup thick caramel topping/filling
milk chocolate curls, made using a vegetable peeler, to decorate

1   Preheat the oven to 160°C (320°F). Line a 24 mini cupcake pan with mini cupcake papers. In a medium-sized bowl, use an electric mixer on high speed to cream the butter and sugar until light and fluffy. Add the egg and mix well.

2   Add the flour, cocoa and milk and beat with an electric mixer on medium until well combined. Stir through white chocolate chips.

3   Divide the mixture evenly between the 24 mini cupcake papers. Bake for 10–15 minutes until well risen and firm to the touch. Allow to cool for a few minutes and then transfer to a wire rack. Allow to cool fully before icing (frosting).

Topping

1   Spoon the caramel onto each cupcake and decorate with chocolate curls.

Makes 24 · Preparation 20 minutes · Cooking 15 minutes

FRUIT & NUT
CUPCAKES

FRUIT & NUT CUPCAKES

Instead of a plate of nuts, serve nutty cupcakes – something different and sure to please. Try the special fruit cupcakes with strawberries, blueberries, apples and dates, all featured in this special chapter.

RASPBERRY COCONUT CUPCAKES

2 eggs
125g (4.4oz) butter, softened
1 cup caster (berry) sugar
½ cup milk
2 tablespoons raspberry liqueur
¼ cup dessicated (fine) coconut
2 cups self-raising flour, sifted
Topping
1 cup icing (confectioner's) sugar
2 tablespoons water
125g (4.4oz) raspberries, to decorate
coconut flakes, to decorate

1   Preheat the oven to 160°C (320°F). Line a 12-cupcake pan with cupcake papers. In a medium-sized bowl, lightly beat the eggs, add butter and sugar, then mix until light and fluffy.

2   Add milk, liqueur, coconut and flour, and stir to combine. Beat with an electric mixer for 2 minutes, until light and creamy.

3   Divide the mixture evenly between the cake papers. Bake for 18–20 minutes until risen and firm to touch. Allow to cool for a few minutes and then transfer to a wire rack. Allow to cool fully before icing (frosting).

Topping

1   Meanwhile, combine icing (confectioner's) sugar and water in a small bowl. Spread icing over each cupcake. Decorate with raspberries and coconut flakes.

Makes 12 • Preparation 12 minutes • Cooking 20 minutes

Lemon poppy cupcakes

2 eggs
125g (4.4oz) butter, softened
1 cup caster (berry) sugar
½ cup Greek-style yoghurt
2 cups self-raising flour, sifted
zest of 2 lemons
juice of 1 lemon
1 teaspoon poppy seeds
Topping
1½ cups icing (confectioner's) sugar
125g (4.4oz) butter, softened
juice of 1 lemon
½ teaspoon poppy seeds
zest of 1 lemon
50g (1.8oz) crystallised (candied) lemon, cut into thin slivers

1   Preheat the oven to 160°C (320°F). Line a 12-cupcake pan with cupcake papers. In a medium-sized bowl, lightly beat the eggs, add butter and sugar, then mix until light and fluffy.

2   Add yoghurt and flour, and stir to combine. Beat with an electric mixer for 2 minutes, until light and creamy. Stir through lemon zest, lemon juice and poppy seeds.

3   Divide the mixture evenly between the cake papers. Bake for 18–20 minutes until risen and firm to touch. Allow to cool for a few minutes and then transfer to a wire rack. Allow to cool fully before icing (frosting).

Topping

1   Meanwhile, combine all the topping ingredients except the crystallised (candied) lemon, mix and spoon onto cakes. Top with crystallised lemon pieces.

Makes 12 · Preparation 12 minutes · Cooking 20 minutes

PEAR AND CINNAMON CUPCAKES

½ pear, peeled and chopped into small pieces
juice of 1 lemon
1 tablespoon cinnamon
2 eggs
125g (4.4oz) butter, softened
1 cup caster (berry) sugar
½ cup milk
2 cups self-raising flour, sifted
Topping
1½ cups icing (confectioner's) sugar
125g (4.4oz) butter, softened
1 tablespoon cinnamon sugar

1 Preheat the oven to 160°C (320°F). Line a 12-cupcake pan with cupcake papers. In a small bowl, coat the pear pieces with lemon juice and sprinkle with cinnamon. In a medium-sized bowl, lightly beat the eggs, add butter and sugar, then mix until light and fluffy.

2 Add milk and flour, and stir to combine. Beat with an electric mixer for 2 minutes, until light and creamy. Add spiced pear and stir through mixture.

3 Divide the mixture evenly between the cake papers. Bake for 18–20 minutes until risen and firm to touch. Allow to cool for a few minutes and then transfer to a wire rack. Allow to cool fully before icing (frosting).

Topping

1 Meanwhile, combine half the icing (confectioner's) sugar and butter, mix with a wooden spoon, add remaining icing sugar and butter and beat with the spoon until light and fluffy. Spoon mixture into piping bag and decorate the top of each cake in a spiral pattern. Sprinkle cinnamon sugar on top.

Makes 12 · Preparation 12 minutes · Cooking 20 minutes

APPLE NUT CUPCAKES

2 eggs
125g (4.4oz) butter, softened
1 cup caster (berry) sugar
½ cup milk
2 cups self-raising flour, sifted
¼ cup smooth peanut butter
1 small green apple, grated
Topping
½ cup caster (berry) sugar, for toffee
1½ cups icing (confectioner's) sugar
125g (4.4oz) butter, softened
2 tablespoons crunchy unsalted peanut butter

1   Preheat the oven to 160°C (320°F). Line a 12-cupcake pan with cupcake papers. In a medium-sized bowl, lightly beat the eggs, add butter and sugar, then mix until light and fluffy.

2   Add milk, flour and peanut butter, and stir to combine. Beat with an electric mixer for 2 minutes, until light and creamy. Add apple and stir through mix.

3   Divide the mixture evenly between the cake papers. Bake for 18–20 minutes until risen and firm to touch. Allow to cool for a few minutes and then transfer to a wire rack. Allow to cool fully before icing (frosting).

Toffee

1   Place caster (berry) sugar evenly on a greaseproof paper–lined baking tray and bake at 200°C for approximately 25 minutes until toffee consistency forms. Cool until hardened.

Topping

1   Meanwhile, combine half the icing (confectioner's) sugar, butter and peanut butter, and mix with a wooden spoon. Add remaining icing sugar, butter and peanut butter and beat with the spoon until light and fluffy.

2   Use the back of a spoon to ice cakes. Top with broken toffee pieces.

Makes 12 · Preparation 12 minutes · Cooking 45 minutes

Sugar plum cupcakes

2 eggs
125g (4.4oz) butter, softened
1 cup caster (berry) sugar
½ cup milk
2 cups self-raising flour, sifted
2 tablespoons plum liqueur
¼ cup chopped plums
Topping
1½ cups icing (confectioner's) sugar
125g (4.4oz) butter, softened
1 drop purple food colouring
sugar (candy) flowers (available from cake decorating shops)

1   Preheat the oven to 160°C (320°F). Line a 12-cupcake pan with cupcake papers. In a medium-sized bowl, lightly beat the eggs, add butter and sugar, then mix until light and fluffy.

2   Add milk, flour and plum liqueur, and stir to combine. Beat with an electric mixer for 5 minutes, until light and creamy, then stir in chopped plums.

3   Divide the mixture evenly between the cake papers. Bake for 18–20 minutes. Allow to cool for a few minutes and then transfer to a wire rack. Allow to cool fully before icing (frosting).

Topping

1   Combine all ingredients except sugar (candy) flowers in a small bowl, mix with a wooden spoon, then whisk until light and fluffy. Place mixture into a piping bag and pipe onto all cupcakes. Decorate with sugar flowers.

Makes 12 · Preparation 12 minutes · Cooking 20 minutes

RUM AND RAISIN MINI CUPCAKES

80g (2.8oz) butter, softened
½ cup caster (berry) sugar
1 egg
1 cup self-raising flour, sifted
⅓ cup milk
½ cup raisins, soaked in 2 tablespoons rum
Topping
80g (2.8oz) butter, softened
1 tablespoon dark rum
1 cup icing (confectioner's) sugar
raisins, to decorate
dark (semi-sweet) chocolate, grated, to decorate

1   Preheat the oven to 160°C (320°F). Line a 24 mini cupcake pan with mini cupcake papers. In a medium-sized bowl, use an electric mixer on high speed to cream the butter and sugar until light and fluffy. Add the egg and mix well.

2   Add the flour and milk and beat with an electric mixer on medium until well combined. Stir through rum-soaked raisins.

3   Divide the mixture evenly between the 24 mini cupcake papers. Bake for 10–15 minutes until well risen and firm to the touch. Allow to cool for a few minutes and then transfer to a wire rack. Allow to cool fully before icing (frosting).

Topping

1   Use an electric mixer on high speed to beat the butter and rum until light and fluffy. Gradually beat in icing (confectioner's) sugar until all combined, continue beating for 1 minute. Use a piping bag fitted with a star nozzle to pipe the icing onto the cupcakes, then decorate with raisins and grated chocolate.

Makes 24 · Preparation 20 minutes · Cooking 15 minutes

Pistachio mini cupcakes

80g (2.8oz) butter, softened
½ cup caster (berry) sugar
1 egg
1 cup self-raising flour, sifted
⅓ cup milk
½ teaspoon vanilla extract
½ cup pistachios, chopped
Topping
80g (2.8oz) butter, softened
1 cup icing (confectioner's) sugar
purple food colouring
whole pistachios, to decorate

1   Preheat the oven to 160°C (320°F). Line a 24 mini cupcake pan with mini cupcake papers. In a medium-sized bowl, use an electric mixer on high speed to cream the butter and sugar until light and fluffy. Add the egg and mix well.

2   Add the flour, milk and vanilla, and beat with an electric mixer on medium until well combined. Stir through pistachios.

3   Divide the mixture evenly between the 24 mini cupcake papers. Bake for 10–15 minutes until well risen and firm to the touch. Allow to cool for a few minutes and then transfer to a wire rack. Allow to cool fully before icing (frosting).

Topping

1   Use an electric mixer on high speed to beat the butter, until light and fluffy. Gradually beat in icing (confectioner's) sugar until all combined, continue beating for 1 minute then tint the icing light purple. Use a piping bag fitted with a star nozzle to pipe the icing onto the cupcakes and decorate with pistachios.

Makes 24 • Preparation 20 minutes • Cooking 15 minutes

BLUEBERRY BLISS MINI CUPCAKES

80g (2.8oz) butter, softened
½ cup caster (berry) sugar
1 egg
1 cup self-raising flour, sifted
⅓ cup milk
½ teaspoon vanilla extract
½ cup fresh blueberries, crushed with a fork
Topping
80g (2.8oz) butter, softened
1 teaspoon vanilla extract
1 cup icing (confectioner's) sugar
blue food colouring
fresh blueberries, to decorate

1   Preheat the oven to 160°C (320°F). Line a 24 mini cupcake pan with mini cupcake papers. In a medium-sized bowl, use an electric mixer on high speed to cream the butter and sugar until light and fluffy. Add the egg and mix well.

2   Add the flour, milk and vanilla, and beat with an electric mixer on medium until well combined. Stir through blueberries.

3   Divide the mixture evenly between the 24 mini cupcake papers. Bake for 10–15 minutes until well risen and firm to the touch. Allow to cool for a few minutes and then transfer to a wire rack. Allow to cool fully before icing (frosting).

Topping

1   Use an electric mixer on high speed to beat the butter and vanilla until light and fluffy. Gradually beat in icing (confectioner's) sugar until all combined. Continue beating for 1 minute then tint the icing light blue. Use a piping bag fitted with a plain nozzle to pipe the icing onto the cupcakes and decorate with blueberries.

Makes 24 · Preparation 20 minutes · Cooking 15 minutes

DATE AND WALNUT MINI CUPCAKES

80g (2.8oz) butter, softened
½ cup caster (berry) sugar
1 egg
1 cup self-raising flour, sifted
⅓ cup milk
½ teaspoon vanilla extract
¼ cup dates, chopped
½ cup walnuts, chopped
Topping
80g (2.8oz) butter, softened
1 teaspoon vanilla extract
1 cup icing (confectioner's) sugar
dates, sliced, to decorate
walnuts, chopped, to decorate

1   Preheat the oven to 160°C (320°F). Line a 24 mini cupcake pan with mini cupcake papers. In a medium-sized bowl, use an electric mixer on high speed to cream the butter and sugar until light and fluffy. Add the egg and mix well.

2   Add the flour, milk and vanilla, and beat with an electric mixer on medium until well combined. Stir through dates and walnuts.

3   Divide the mixture evenly between the 24 mini cupcake papers. Bake for 10–15 minutes until well risen and firm to the touch. Allow to cool for a few minutes and then transfer to a wire rack. Allow to cool fully before icing (frosting).

Topping

1   Use an electric mixer on high speed to beat the butter and vanilla, until light and fluffy. Gradually beat in icing (confectioner's) sugar until all combined, then continue beating for 1 minute. Use a piping bag fitted with a star nozzle to pipe the icing onto the cupcakes and decorate with dates and walnuts.

Makes 24 • Preparation 20 minutes • Cooking 15 minutes

Peach Melba mini cupcakes

80g (2.8oz) butter, softened
½ cup caster (berry) sugar
1 egg
1 cup self-raising flour, sifted
⅓ cup milk
½ teaspoon vanilla extract
¼ cup fresh raspberries, crushed with a fork
¼ cup canned peaches, drained and diced
Topping
80g (2.8oz) butter, softened
1 cup icing (confectioner's) sugar
¼ cup canned peaches, diced
fresh raspberries, to decorate

1 Preheat the oven to 160°C (320°F). Line a 24 mini cupcake pan with mini cupcake papers. In a medium-sized bowl, use an electric mixer on high speed to cream the butter and sugar until light and fluffy. Add the egg and mix well.

2 Add the flour, milk and vanilla, and beat with an electric mixer on medium until well combined. Stir through raspberries and peaches.

3 Divide the mixture evenly between the 24 mini cupcake papers. Bake for 10–15 minutes until well risen and firm to the touch. Allow to cool for a few minutes and then transfer to a wire rack. Allow to cool fully before icing (frosting).

Topping

1 Use an electric mixer on high speed to beat the butter, until light and fluffy. Gradually beat in icing (confectioner's) sugar until all combined, continue beating for 1 minute. Stir through peaches. Spread evenly over each cupcake and decorate with fresh raspberries.

Makes 24 · Preparation 20 minutes · Cooking 15 minutes

CHERRY MACADAMIA MINI CUPCAKES

80g (2.8oz) butter, softened
½ cup caster (berry) sugar
1 egg
1 cup self-raising flour, sifted
⅓ cup milk
½ teaspoon vanilla extract
¼ cup glacé (glazed) cherries, chopped
¼ cup macadamia nuts, chopped
Topping
80g (2.8oz) butter, softened
1 cup icing (confectioner's) sugar
pink food colouring
¼ cup macadamia nuts, chopped
glacé (glazed) cherries, to decorate

1   Preheat the oven to 160°C (320°F). Line a 24 mini cupcake pan with mini cupcake papers. In a medium-sized bowl, use an electric mixer on high speed to cream the butter and sugar until light and fluffy. Add the egg and mix well.

2   Add the flour, milk and vanilla, and beat with an electric mixer on medium until well combined. Stir through cherries and macadamia nuts.

3   Divide the mixture evenly between the 24 mini cupcake papers. Bake for 10–15 minutes until well risen and firm to the touch. Allow to cool for a few minutes and then transfer to a wire rack. Allow to cool fully before icing (frosting).

Topping

1   Use an electric mixer on high speed to beat the butter, until light and fluffy. Gradually beat in icing (confectioner's) sugar until all combined, continue beating for 1 minute, tint icing pink and stir in macadamia nuts. Spread evenly over each cupcake and decorate with cherries.

Makes 24 · Preparation 20 minutes · Cooking 15 minutes

BANANA AND WALNUT MINI CUPCAKES

80g (2.8oz) butter, softened
½ cup caster (berry) sugar
1 egg
1 cup self-raising flour, sifted
⅓ cup milk
½ teaspoon vanilla extract
¼ cup banana, mashed
¼ cup walnuts, chopped
Topping
80g (2.8oz) butter, softened
1 teaspoon vanilla extract
1 cup icing (confectioner's) sugar
walnuts, chopped, to decorate

1 Preheat the oven to 160°C (320°F). Line a 24 mini cupcake pan with mini cupcake papers. In a medium-sized bowl, use an electric mixer on high speed to cream the butter and sugar until light and fluffy. Add the egg and mix well.

2 Add the flour, milk and vanilla, and beat with an electric mixer on medium until well combined. Stir in mashed banana and walnuts.

3 Divide the mixture evenly between the 24 mini cupcake papers. Bake for 10–15 minutes until well risen and firm to the touch. Allow to cool for a few minutes and then transfer to a wire rack. Allow to cool fully before icing (frosting).

Topping

1 Use an electric mixer on high speed to beat the butter and vanilla until light and fluffy. Gradually beat in icing (confectioner's) sugar until all combined, then continue beating for 1 minute. Use a piping bag fitted with a star nozzle to pipe icing onto cupcakes and decorate with chopped walnuts.

Makes 24 · Preparation 20 minutes · Cooking 15 minutes

Peanut butter mini cupcakes

80g (2.8oz) butter, softened
½ cup caster (berry) sugar
1 egg
1 cup self-raising flour, sifted
⅓ cup milk
½ teaspoon vanilla extract
¼ cup peanut butter
Topping
80g (2.8oz) butter, softened
1 cup icing (confectioner's) sugar
¼ cup crunchy peanut butter
roasted peanuts, chopped, to decorate

1   Preheat the oven to 160°C (320°F). Line a 24 mini cupcake pan with mini cupcake papers. In a medium-sized bowl, use an electric mixer on high speed to cream the butter and sugar until light and fluffy. Add the egg and mix well.

2   Add the flour, milk and vanilla, and beat with an electric mixer on medium until well combined. Stir in peanut butter.

3   Divide the mixture evenly between the 24 mini cupcake papers. Bake for 10–15 minutes until well risen and firm to the touch. Allow to cool for a few minutes and then transfer to a wire rack. Allow to cool fully before icing (frosting).

Topping

1   Use an electric mixer on high speed to beat the butter until light and fluffy. Gradually beat in icing (confectioner's) sugar until all combined, continue beating for 1 minute then stir in the peanut butter. Use a piping bag fitted with a star nozzle to pipe icing onto cupcakes and decorate with roasted peanuts.

Makes 24 · Preparation 20 minutes · Cooking 15 minutes

CITRUS CUPCAKES

CITRUS CUPCAKES

The tartness and strong acidic qualities of citrus fruits often need a helping hand from something sweet for them to mellow into a delicious dessert. The two flavours work exceptionally well in this chapter.

LEMON CARROT WALNUT CUPCAKES

2 eggs
1 cup caster (berry) sugar
¾ cup vegetable oil
½ cup lemon juice
2 cups plain (all-purpose) flour
1 teaspoon ground cinnamon
2 teaspoons baking powder
½ teaspoon ground cloves
¾ cup carrot, grated
zest of 1 lemon
½ cup walnut pieces
Topping
1½ cups icing (confectioner's) sugar
zest 1 lemon
1 teaspoon lemon juice
90g (3.2oz) butter, softened
1 drop orange food colouring
½ cup walnut pieces

1　Preheat the oven to 180°C (350°F). Line a 12-cupcake pan with cupcake papers. In a medium-sized bowl, beat eggs, sugar, oil and lemon juice with an electric mixer until thoroughly combined and creamy.

2　Sift all dry ingredients except walnuts into a bowl, then add to egg mixture. Beat mixture for five minutes, then add the carrot and lemon zest and stir to combine. Fold through walnuts.

3　Divide the mixture evenly between the cake cases. Bake for 20–25 minutes. Transfer to a wire rack. Allow to cool fully before icing (frosting).

Topping

1　Meanwhile, combine topping ingredients except the walnuts, and beat with an electric mixer for 5 minutes until creamy. Use a spatula to apply topping to each cupcake and top with walnut pieces.

Makes 12 · Preparation 15 minutes · Cooking 25 minutes

GINGER ZINGER CUPCAKES

2 eggs
125g (4.4oz) butter, softened
1 cup caster (berry) sugar
½ cup buttermilk
2 cups self-raising flour, sifted
½ cup crystallised (candied) ginger, finely chopped
juice of ½ lemon
zest of 1 lemon
Topping
1 cup icing (confectioner's) sugar
2 tablespoons lemon juice
50g (1.7oz) glacé (glazed) ginger

1. Preheat the oven to 160°C (320°F). Line a 12-cupcake pan with cupcake papers. In a medium-sized bowl, lightly beat the eggs, add butter and sugar, then mix until light and fluffy.

2. Add buttermilk and flour, and stir to combine. Beat with an electric mixer for 2 minutes, until light and creamy. Add crystallised (candied) ginger, lemon juice and zest, and mix thoroughly.

3. Divide the mixture evenly between the cake papers. Bake for 18–20 minutes until risen and firm to touch. Allow to cool for a few minutes and then transfer to a wire rack. Allow to cool fully before icing (frosting).

Topping

1. Mix icing (confectioner's) sugar with enough lemon juice to make a smooth paste. Spread evenly over the cupcakes. Top with slices of glacé (glazed) ginger.

Makes 12 · Preparation 12 minutes · Cooking 20 minutes

CITRUS BURST CUPCAKES

2 eggs
1 cup caster (berry) sugar
½ cup vegetable oil
¼ cup lemon juice
zest of 1 lemon
zest of 1 lime
2 cups plain (all-purpose) flour
2 teaspoons baking powder
½ cup almond meal
Topping
1½ cups icing (confectioner's) sugar
zest of 1 lemon
1 teaspoon lemon juice
90g (3.2oz) butter, softened
crystallised (candied) lime, lemon and orange zest to decorate

1   Preheat the oven to 180°C (350°F). Line a 12-cupcake pan with cupcake papers.
    In a medium-sized bowl, beat eggs, sugar, oil, lemon juice and zests with an electric
    mixer until thoroughly combined and creamy.

2   Sift the flour and baking powder into a bowl, then add the almond meal and lemon
    and egg mixture, and beat for 5 minutes.

3   Divide the mixture evenly between the cake papers. Bake for 20–25 minutes.
    Allow to cool for a few minutes and then transfer to a wire rack. Allow to cool
    fully before icing (frosting).

Topping

1   Meanwhile, combine all ingredients except the citrus zest and beat with an electric
    mixer for 5 minutes until creamy. Apply the topping to cupcakes. Sprinkle with
    mixed zests.

Makes 12 · Preparation 15 minutes · Cooking 25 minutes

PINK GRAPEFRUIT CUPCAKES

2 eggs
125g (4.4oz) butter, softened
1 cup caster (berry) sugar
½ cup yoghurt
2 tablespoons grapefruit juice
zest of 1 pink grapefruit
2 cups self-raising flour, sifted
1 teaspoon vanilla extract
Topping
1½ cups icing (confectioner's) sugar
125g (4.4oz) butter, softened
2 tablespoons pink grapefruit juice
1–2 drops pink colouring

1   Preheat the oven to 160°C (320°F). Line a 12-cupcake pan with cupcake papers. In a medium-sized bowl, lightly beat the eggs, add butter and sugar, then mix until light and fluffy.

2   Add yoghurt, grapefruit juice, grapefruit zest, flour and vanilla, and stir to combine. Beat with an electric mixer for 2 minutes, until light and creamy.

3   Divide the mixture evenly between the cake papers. Bake for 18–20 minutes until risen and firm to touch. Allow to cool for a few minutes and then transfer to a wire rack. Allow to cool fully before icing (frosting).

Topping

1   Meanwhile, combine half the icing (confectioner's) sugar and butter, mix with a wooden spoon, add remaining sugar and butter and beat with the spoon until light and fluffy. Mix in pink grapefruit juice and colouring. Spread onto cupcakes.

Makes 12 · Preparation 12 minutes · Cooking 20 minutes

CHERRY SOUR CREAM BUTTER CUPCAKES

125g (4.4oz) butter, softened
1 teaspoon vanilla extract
zest of 1 large lemon
1 cup caster (berry) sugar
2 eggs
2 cups self-raising flour, sifted
⅓ cup sour cream
¼ cup chopped morello cherries
Topping
1½ cups icing (confectioner's) sugar
zest of 1 lemon
½ teaspoon lemon juice
125g (4.4oz) butter, softened
morello cherries, to decorate

1   Preheat the oven to 160°C (320°F). Line a 12-cupcake pan with cupcake papers. In a bowl, beat the butter, vanilla, lemon zest and sugar with an electric mixer until light and fluffy.

2   Beat in the eggs one at a time, scraping down the bowl between additions. Stir in half the flour and sour cream. Blend well. Mix in the remaining flour and sour cream, and mix thoroughly but gently. Stir in cherries.

3   Divide the mixture evenly between the cake papers. Bake for 18–20 minutes until risen and firm to touch. Allow to cool for a few minutes and then transfer to a wire rack. Allow to cool fully before icing (frosting).

Topping

1   Meanwhile, combine all ingredients except cherries and beat with an electric mixer for 5 minutes until creamy. Spoon mixture into a piping bag and decorate the top of each cake in a spiral pattern. Top with cherries.

Makes 12 · Preparation 15 minutes · Cooking 20 minutes

CHOC ORANGE CUPCAKES

2 eggs
125g (4.4oz) butter, softened
1 cup caster (berry) sugar
½ cup milk
2 cups self-raising flour, sifted
1 teaspoon cocoa powder
1 teaspoon vanilla extract
juice of 1 orange
zest of 1 orange
¼ cup chocolate chips or flakes
Topping
2 cups icing (confectioner's) sugar
125g (4.4oz) butter, softened
¼ cup orange juice
crushed chocolate orange balls, to decorate

1   Preheat the oven to 160°C (320°F). Line a 12-cupcake pan with cupcake papers. In a medium-sized bowl, lightly beat the eggs, add butter and sugar, then mix until light and fluffy.

2   Add milk, flour, cocoa powder and vanilla, and stir to combine. Beat with an electric mixer for 2 minutes, until light and creamy. Add juice, zest and chocolate chips, and stir to combine.

3   Divide the mixture evenly between the cake papers. Bake for 18–20 minutes until risen and firm to touch. Allow to cool for a few minutes and then transfer to a wire rack. Allow to cool fully before icing (frosting).

Topping

1   Meanwhile, combine half of all the topping ingredients except chocolate balls, mix with a wooden spoon, add remaining ingredients except chocolate balls and beat with the spoon until light and fluffy. Use a piping bag fitted with a star nozzle to pipe the icing onto the cupcakes. Top with chocolate ball pieces.

Makes 12 · Preparation 12 minutes · Cooking 20 minutes

Lemon and lime cupcakes

2 cups self-raising flour, sifted
1 cup caster (berry) sugar
125g (4.4oz) butter, softened
2 eggs
½ cup buttermilk
1 teaspoon lemon extract
1 teaspoon lime extract
zest of 1 lime
zest of 1 lemon
Sugared citrus zest
zest of 3 limes
zest of 3 lemons
¾ cup caster (berry) sugar
Topping
125g (4.4oz) unsalted butter, softened
½ teaspoon lime extract
½ teaspoon lemon extract
1½ cups icing (confectioner's) sugar

1   Preheat the oven to 180°C (350°F). Line a 12-cupcake pan with cupcake papers. Place all the ingredients except the zests in a bowl, and beat with an electric mixer for 5 minutes until pale and fluffy. Fold in the zests.

2   Divide the mixture evenly between the cake papers. Bake for 20–25 minutes until risen and firm to touch. Allow to cool for a few minutes and then transfer to a wire rack. Allow to cool fully before icing (frosting).

Sugared citrus zest

1   Meanwhile, to make the sugared citrus zest, coat the lime and lemon zest with caster (berry) sugar and toss to thoroughly combine. Leave for at least 10 minutes.

Topping

2   Beat the butter with an electric mixer for 2 minutes and add extracts and half of the icing (confectioner's) sugar. Beat for 3 minutes. Add the rest of the sugar and beat for a further 3 minutes.

3   Add mixture to piping bag, pipe onto cakes and top with the sugared citrus zest.

Makes 12 • Preparation 35 minutes • Cooking 25 minutes

NOVELTY
CUPCAKES

NOVELTY CUPCAKES

No cupcake book would be complete without a set of playful recipes reminding you of all the celebrations that cupcakes can help you with. Keep a supply of assorted sugar decorations on hand for making up a batch of novelty cupcakes for any celebration.

Baby cupcakes

2 eggs
125g (4.4oz) butter, softened
1 cup caster (berry) sugar
½ cup milk
2 cups self-raising flour, sifted
1 teaspoon vanilla extract
Topping
1½ cups icing (confectioner's) sugar
125g (4.4oz) butter, softened
1 tablespoon water
6 drops blue or pink food colouring
3 teaspoons coloured sugar sprinkles

1 Preheat the oven to 160°C (320°F). Line a 12-cupcake pan with cupcake papers. In a medium-sized bowl, lightly beat the eggs, add butter and sugar, then mix until light and fluffy.

2 Add milk, flour and vanilla, and stir to combine. Beat with an electric mixer for 2 minutes, until light and creamy.

3 Divide the mixture evenly between the cake papers. Bake for 18–20 minutes until risen and firm to touch. Allow to cool for a few minutes and then transfer to a wire rack. Allow to cool fully before icing (frosting).

Topping

1 Meanwhile, thoroughly combine the topping ingredients. Using the back of a teaspoon, apply the topping to cupcakes. Top with sugar sprinkles.

Makes 12 · Preparation 12 minutes · Cooking 20 minutes

Angel wing cupcakes

2 eggs
125g (4.4oz) butter, softened
1 cup caster (berry) sugar
½ cup milk
2 cups self-raising flour, sifted
1 teaspoon vanilla extract
Topping
1 cup whipped cream
¼ cup raspberry jam
½ cup icing (confectioner's) sugar
1 tablespoon water
sprinkles, to decorate

1   Preheat the oven to 160°C (320°F). Line a 12-cupcake pan with cupcake papers. In a medium-sized bowl, lightly beat the eggs, add butter and sugar, then mix until light and fluffy.

2   Add milk, flour and vanilla, and stir to combine. Beat with an electric mixer for 2 minutes, until light and creamy.

3   Divide the mixture evenly between the cake papers. Bake for 18–20 minutes until risen and firm to touch. Allow to cool for a few minutes and then transfer to a wire rack. Allow to cool fully before icing (frosting).

Topping

1   Place cream into a piping bag and set aside. Using a sharp knife, cut a 10cm circle into the centre of each cupcake, slicing the top off. Cut these circles in half and set aside. Fill the centre of each cupcake with cream and top with a small amount of jam.

2   Mix together icing (confectioner's) sugar and enough water to form a smooth paste. Spread each wing with icing and top with sprinkles.

3   Stand the two half-circles of cake upright, to form wings.

Makes 12 · Preparation 12 minutes · Cooking 20 minutes

Springtime cupcakes

2 eggs
125g (4.4oz) butter, softened
1 cup caster (berry) sugar
½ cup milk
2 cups self-raising flour, sifted
1 teaspoon vanilla extract
½ teaspoon yellow food colouring
zest of 1 lemon
Topping
1½ cups icing (confectioner's) sugar
125g (4.4oz) butter, softened
2 drops yellow food colouring
sugar (candy) flowers (available from cake decoration stores)

1   Preheat the oven to 160°C (320°F). Line a 12-cupcake pan with cupcake papers. In a medium-sized bowl, lightly beat the eggs, add butter and sugar, then mix until light and fluffy.

2   Add milk, flour, vanilla and yellow food colouring, stir to combine. Beat with an electric mixer for 2 minutes, until light and creamy, then stir through the zest.

3   Divide the mixture evenly between the cake papers. Bake for 18–20 minutes until risen and firm to touch. Allow to cool for a few minutes and then transfer to a wire rack. Allow to cool fully before icing (frosting).

Topping

1   Meanwhile, combine all the topping ingredients, except the flowers, and mix well with a wooden spoon.

2   Using the back of a teaspoon, apply icing to each cupcake. Top each cupcake with sugar (candy) flowers.

Makes 12 · Preparation 12 minutes · Cooking 20 minutes

EASTER NEST CUPCAKES

2 eggs
125g (4.4oz) butter, softened
1 cup caster (berry) sugar
½ cup milk
2 cups self-raising flour, sifted
1 teaspoon vanilla extract
100g (3.5oz) dark (semi-sweet) chocolate pieces
1 tablespoon cocoa powder
Topping
100g (3.5oz) dark (semi-sweet) chocolate
1 tablespoon butter, softened
⅓ cup thickened (whipping) cream
½ cup butter, softened
1½ cups icing (confectioner's) sugar
flaked chocolate, to decorate
12 small Easter eggs, to decorate

1   Preheat the oven to 160°C (320°F). Line a 12-cupcake pan with cupcake papers. In a medium-sized bowl, lightly beat the eggs, add butter and sugar, then mix until light and fluffy.

2   Add milk, flour and vanilla, and stir to combine. Add remaining ingredients. Beat with an electric mixer for 2 minutes, until light and creamy.

3   Divide the mixture evenly between the cake papers. Bake for 18–20 minutes until risen and firm to touch. Allow to cool for a few minutes and then transfer to a wire rack. Allow to cool fully before icing (frosting).

Topping

1   Meanwhile, combine the chocolate and tablespoon of butter in a medium-sized saucepan over medium heat. As the mixture begins to melt, add cream slowly, then reduce heat to low, stirring constantly until mixture thickens. Remove from heat and cool.

2   Combine butter and icing (confectioner's) sugar, mix with a wooden spoon, then beat with the spoon until light and fluffy. Add melted chocolate and combine. Spoon onto cupcakes and make small nests out of the flaked chocolate. Place an egg in each nest.

Makes 12 • Preparation 12 minutes • Cooking 20 minutes

ANIMAL CUPCAKES

2 eggs
125g (4.4oz) butter, softened
1 cup caster (berry) sugar
½ cup milk
2 cups self-raising flour, sifted
1 teaspoon vanilla extract
Topping
1 cup icing (confectioner's) sugar
2 tablepoons water
food colouring of choice
confectionary animals

1   Preheat the oven to 160°C (320°F). Line a 12-cupcake pan with cupcake papers. In a medium-sized bowl, lightly beat the eggs, add butter and sugar, then mix until light and fluffy.

2   Add milk, flour and vanilla, and stir to combine. Beat with an electric mixer for 2 minutes, until light and creamy.

3   Divide the mixture evenly between the cake papers. Bake for 18–20 minutes until risen and firm to touch. Allow to cool for a few minutes and then transfer to a wire rack. Allow to cool fully before icing (frosting).

Topping

1   Mix icing (confectioner's) sugar with enough water to make a smooth paste. Divide into 4 equal bowls and tint each one a different colour. Ice cupcakes and top each with confectionary animals.

Makes 12 • Preparation 12 minutes • Cooking 20 minutes

VANILLA CANDY CANE CUPCAKES

2 eggs
125g (4.4oz) butter, softened
1 cup caster (berry) sugar
½ cup milk
2 cups self-raising flour, sifted
2 teaspoons vanilla extract
Topping
100g (3.5oz) dark (semi-sweet) chocolate
1 tablespoon butter, softened
⅓ cup thickened (whipping) cream
mini candy canes, to decorate

1   Preheat the oven to 160°C (320°F). Line a 12-cupcake pan with cupcake papers. In a medium-sized bowl, lightly beat the eggs, add butter and sugar, then mix until light and fluffy.

2   Add milk, flour and vanilla, and stir to combine. Beat with an electric mixer for 2 minutes, until light and creamy.

3   Divide the mixture evenly between the cake papers. Bake for 18–20 minutes until risen and firm to touch. Allow to cool for a few minutes and then transfer to a wire rack. Allow to cool fully before icing (frosting).

Topping

1   Meanwhile, combine the chocolate and butter in a medium-sized saucepan over medium heat. As the mixture begins to melt, reduce heat to low and add cream slowly, stirring constantly until the mixture thickens. Remove from heat and cool. Decorate the top of each cake with topping and candy canes.

Makes 12 · Preparation 12 minutes · Cooking 20 minutes

SANTA TOP CUPCAKES

3 eggs
125g (4.4oz) unsalted butter, softened
½ cup caster (berry) sugar
⅓ cup unsweetened pineapple juice
1 cup plain (all-purpose) flour, sifted
1½ cups crystallised (candied) fruit, finely chopped
⅔ cup raisins, chopped
¼ cup pitted dates, finely chopped
¾ teaspoon baking powder
½ teaspoon salt
½ teaspoon vanilla extract
Topping
1½ cups icing (confectioner's) sugar
1 teaspoon lemon extract
125g (4.4oz) butter, softened
1 tablespoon brandy
sugar (candy) novelty Christmas decorations

1   Preheat the oven to 160°C (320°F). Line a 12-cupcake pan with cupcake papers. In a medium-sized bowl, lightly beat the eggs, add butter and sugar, then mix until light and fluffy.

2   Add pineapple juice and flour, and stir to combine. Add remaining ingredients. Beat with an electric mixer for 2 minutes, until light and creamy.

3   Divide the mixture evenly between the cake papers. Bake for 18–20 minutes until risen and firm to touch. Allow to cool for a few minutes and then transfer to a wire rack. Allow to cool fully before icing (frosting).

Topping

1   Meanwhile, combine half-quantities of all the topping ingredients, except for the novelty decorations, and mix with a wooden spoon. Add remaining half and beat with the spoon until light and fluffy.

2   Put icing into a piping bag with a medium-sized plain nozzle and pipe onto cupcakes. Top with novelty decorations.

Makes 12 · Preparation 12 minutes · Cooking 20 minutes

SUMMER FUN CUPCAKES

2 cups self-raising flour, sifted
½ cup caster (berry) sugar
½ cup soft brown sugar
1 teaspoon ground cinnamon
1 teaspoon salt
150ml (5fl oz) sunflower oil
2 eggs, beaten
200g (7oz) canned pineapple chunks, drained and chopped
Topping
275g (9.7oz) icing (confectioner's) sugar, sifted
125g (4.4oz) mascarpone
4 teaspoons lemon juice
2 drops vanilla extract
1 box yellow fondant icing
tube of black gel icing

1   Preheat the oven to 180°C (350°F). Line two 12-cupcake pans with cupcake papers. Using a wooden spoon, mix the flour, sugars, cinnamon and salt. Add the oil and eggs and beat until thoroughly combined. Mix in the pineapple and beat well.

2   Divide the mixture evenly between the cake papers. Bake for 18–20 minutes until risen and firm to touch. Allow to cool for a few minutes and then transfer to a wire rack. Allow to cool fully before icing (frosting).

Topping

1   Meanwhile, mix the icing (confectioner's) sugar, mascarpone, lemon juice and vanilla extract with a fork until smooth. Spread over the cakes.

2   Cut out sun shapes from the yellow fondant. Place on top of cupcakes and use the gel icing to pipe happy faces on the suns.

Makes 24 • Preparation 30 minutes • Cooking 20 minutes

WEIGHTS AND MEASURES

Although recipes have been tested using the Australian Standard 250ml cup, 20ml tablespoon and 5ml teaspoon, they will work just as well with the US and Canadian 8fl oz cup, or the UK 300ml cup. We have used graduated cup measures in preference to tablespoon measures so that proportions are always the same. Where tablespoon measures have been given, they are not crucial measures, so using the smaller tablespoon of the US or UK will not affect the recipe's success. But we all agree on the teaspoon size.

For breads, cakes and pastries, the only area which might cause concern is where eggs are used, as proportions will then vary. If working with a 250ml or 300ml cup, use large eggs (65g/2¼oz), adding a little more liquid to the recipe for 300ml cup measures if it seems necessary. Use medium-sized eggs (55g/2oz) with an 8fl oz cup measure. A graduated set of measuring cups and spoons is recommended, the cups in particular for measuring dry ingredients. Remember to level such ingredients to ensure an accurate quantity.

Oven Temperatures

The Celsius temperatures given here are not exact; they have been rounded off and are given as a guide only. Follow the manufacturer's temperature guide, relating it to oven description given in the recipe. Remember gas ovens are hottest at the top, electric ovens at the bottom and convection-fan forced ovens are usually even throughout. We've included Regulo numbers for gas cookers, which may assist. To convert °C to °F multiply °C by 9 and divide by 5 then add 32.

	C°	F°	Gas Regulo
Very slow	120	250	1
Slow	150	300	2
Moderately slow	160	320	3
Moderate	180	350	4
Moderately hot	190–200	370–400	5–6
Hot	210–220	410–440	6–7
Very hot	230	450	8
Super hot	250–290	475–500	9–10

English Measures

English measurements are similar to Australian with two exceptions: the English cup measures 300ml/10½fl oz, whereas the American and Australian cup measure 250ml/8¾fl oz. The English tablespoon (the Australian dessertspoon) measures 14.8ml/½ fl oz against the Australian tablespoon of 20ml/¾fl oz. The Imperial measurement is 20fl oz to the pint, 40fl oz a quart and 160fl oz per gallon.

American Measures

The American reputed pint is 16fl oz, a quart is equal to 32fl oz and the American gallon, 128fl oz. The American tablespoon is equal to 14.8ml/½fl oz, the teaspoon is 5ml/⅙fl oz. The cup measure is 250ml/8¾fl oz.

Dry Measures

All the measures are level, so when you have filled a cup or spoon, level it off with the edge of a knife. The scale opposite is the 'cook's equivalent'; it is not an exact conversion of metric to imperial measurement. To calculate the exact metric equivalent yourself, multiply ounces by 28.349523 to obtain grams, or divide grams by 28.349523 to obtain ounces.

Metric grams (g), kilograms (kg)	Imperial ounces (oz), pound (lb)	Metric grams (g), kilograms (kg)	Imperial ounces (oz), pound (lb)
15g	$\frac{1}{2}$oz	225g	8oz/$\frac{1}{2}$lb
20g	$\frac{2}{3}$oz	315g	11oz
30g	1oz	340g	12oz/$\frac{3}{4}$lb
55g	2oz	370g	13oz
85g	3oz	400g	14oz
115g	4oz/$\frac{1}{4}$lb	425g	15oz
125g	4$\frac{1}{2}$oz	455g	16oz/1lb
140/145g	5oz	1000g/1kg	35.3oz/2$\frac{1}{5}$lb
170g	6oz	1$\frac{1}{2}$kg	3$\frac{1}{3}$lb
200g	7oz		

Liquid Measures

Metric millilitres (ml)	Imperial fluid ounce (fl oz)	Cup and Spoon
5ml	$\frac{1}{6}$fl oz	1 teaspoon
20ml	$\frac{2}{3}$fl oz	1 tablespoon
30ml	1fl oz	1 tbsp + 2 tsp
55ml	2fl oz	
63ml	2$\frac{1}{4}$fl oz	$\frac{1}{4}$ cup
85ml	3fl oz	
115ml	4fl oz	
125ml	4$\frac{1}{2}$fl oz	$\frac{1}{2}$ cup
150ml	5$\frac{1}{4}$fl oz	
188ml	6$\frac{2}{3}$fl oz	$\frac{3}{4}$ cup
225ml	8fl oz	
250ml	8fl oz	1 cup
300ml	10$\frac{1}{2}$fl oz	
370ml	13fl oz	
400ml	14fl oz	
438ml	15$\frac{1}{2}$fl oz	1$\frac{3}{4}$ cups
455ml	16fl oz	
500ml	17$\frac{1}{2}$fl oz	2 cups
570ml	20fl oz	
1 litre	35$\frac{1}{3}$fl oz	4 cups

INDEX